CANDIDATES FOR OFFICE

Beliefs and Strategies

STUDIES IN
POLITICAL
SCIENCE

CANDIDATES FOR OFFICE

Beliefs and Strategies

JOHN W. KINGDON

University of Michigan

Random House • *New York*

329
K54c

To my parents

PREFACE

This book deals with politicians' beliefs about voters, their views of coalition building, their sources of information, their campaign strategies, and the implications of these matters for our understanding of the relationships between people and politicians in democracies. It is based on personal interviews conducted with a probability sample of successful and unsuccessful Wisconsin candidates in the 1964 election for offices ranging from United States senator and governor to the lower house of the state legislature.

The study began as a Ph.D. dissertation at the University of Wisconsin. I owe a great debt of gratitude to Ralph Huitt, who helped me avoid many pitfalls during the design of the project and throughout my graduate student days, and to Austin Ranney and Leon Epstein, who contributed their wise counsel from the beginning of this study. Many others—students, colleagues, and mentors—have offered their help and criticisms throughout the research and writing of this volume. In particular, I very much appreciate the care with which H. Douglas Price, Lewis Dexter, Lewis Froman, and James Eisenstein read an earlier version of the manuscript and the comments they offered. Donald Stokes, Philip Converse, Warren Miller, Jack Walker, Robert Schoenberger, and Keith Ovenden criticized portions of the manuscript. They have all improved the final product.

I also benefited greatly from the help given me by Harry Sharp and his staff at the University of Wisconsin Survey Research Laboratory. Merrill Shanks and Bert Wagner gave freely of their skill and advice in the computer work. Editors at Random House, including Anne Murphy and Jeannine Ciliotta, have contributed greatly to the readability of the book. Mary Lou Gaul and Kathy Madison helped by typing at various stages.

The study was made possible financially by a fellowship from the graduate school at the University of Wisconsin and grants from the Institute of Public Administration and the Brownell Fund at the University of Michigan. I wish to thank *The American Political Science Review* for permission to reprint material from my article, "Politicians' Beliefs about Voters," 61 (1967), pp. 137–45, in Chapter 2.

My greatest debts are owed to the seventy candidates with whom I talked, who gave so generously of their time and thoughts, and to my wife Kirsten, who typed, edited, commented, and provided constant and warm companionship.

Ann Arbor, Michigan   J.W.K.

CONTENTS

CANDIDATES FOR OFFICE

Beliefs and Strategies

Chapter 1

INTRODUCTION: THE STUDY AND ITS SETTING

This is a book about the relationships between politicians and those in the democratic system whom they strive to represent. It deals with politicians' beliefs about their constituents, the sorts of information they use to formulate these beliefs, and the strategies they adopt in order to gain and retain elective office. The book is based on data gathered by personal interviews with a sample of successful and unsuccessful Wisconsin candidates in the 1964 election for offices ranging from United States senator and governor to member of the lower house of the state legislature.

This subject of candidates' beliefs and strategies is central to our understanding of the functioning of democratic political systems. For years men have theorized about democracies. Much of this theory has been essentially normative, prescribing a process by which the wishes of the people are somehow translated into government policy, or at least a process by which the passive consent of the governed is obtained. Intimately bound with this concern is a specific mechanism for securing this responsiveness of governmental policy-makers to the people: a system of representation in which governmental policy is made by representatives chosen by the people in free elections. Indeed, some have argued that this mechanism of elections is the defining characteristic of a democracy.[1]

From a descriptive point of view, the simplest statement of the representative relationship is a model with only two elements: the behavior of the representative on the one hand and the wishes of the people on the other. Every theory of representation—complex or simple, normative or descriptive—is concerned with the relationship between these two elements.

Social scientists have learned a good deal about the element in this model that one might label "the people." there is an impressive array of literature designed to discover the attitudes of rank-and-file voters, their degree of involvement and participation in politics, many of their ways of thinking, and explanations for their behavior in the voting booth. Thanks to the work of Bernard R. Berelson and Paul F. Lazarsfeld,[2] V. O. Key, Jr.,[3] and especially of scholars at the University of Michigan Survey Research Center,[4] we know a good deal about the behavior of voters. From surveys of the public we have learned not only about the behavior of voters, but also more generally about reasons for political participation, socialization of people into politics, learning of political attitudes—phenomena that reach beyond the act of voting to more general propositions about human behavior as it is relevant to political life.

Compared with our knowledge of the behavior of the mass public, we know less about the second element in the simple model of democracy: the politicians. Most of the readers of this book are familiar with politicians in some way—perhaps through the news media or through personal contact. Relatively little systematic empirical research, however, has been conducted to discover the reasons why politicians behave as they do vis-à-vis their constituents. What makes the politician tick? We know little in answer to such a question.

It is hoped that the research presented here, which focuses on politicians' cognitions about the election process, will contribute to an answer. One of the basic tenets of democracy is that elections and the anticipation of elections by governmental policy-makers are crucial mechanisms by which the nonleaders in the system can control the leaders. Elections are also a principal means of determining who will rule, whose views will prevail. Campaigning and the election process itself are the basic concerns of this book. But because elections are so central to democratic political systems, the findings presented here may also have implications, which we will discuss, for fundamental questions of governmental policy-making and representation in democracies.

THE SETTING OF THIS STUDY

Literature on the relationships between politicians and their constituents is growing, and it is in this body of works that the present study belongs. A brief topical outline of some of the kinds of writing already done concerning these relationships will help to indicate the intellectual setting for this book. In the process it will become evident how the original, simplest model of politician-constituent interaction has become elaborated.

One type of research has been concentrated on the direct relationship between the district and the politician. Although in such scholarship an assumption may be made that various kinds of processes intervene between the leader and his constituents, the intervening mechanisms themselves have not been examined directly. This type of literature is exemplified by the many roll call studies that have related constituency characteristics to roll call voting in legislatures. These studies include Julius Turner's pioneering work on the importance of party and constituency in roll call voting, the major studies of David E. Truman on political parties in Congress and of Duncan MacRae, Jr., on issue dimensions of congressional voting, and the more recent work of Lewis A. Froman, Jr., which related such district variables as percentage of nonwhite constituents and urbanization to roll call votes in Congress.[5] This research may consider to an extent the mental characteristics of the representative, such as his perceptions of his constituency and his values concerning the proper role of the representative, but its thrust is the direct relationship between constituency and vote without explicit data on the cognitive processes of the politician that link people and government.

The results that appear in much of this literature on the direct relationship between constituency and roll call vote have led to the conclusion that the political party of the representative is more important in his voting than the character of his constituency. Unfortunately, this finding does not settle the question of constituency influence on the legislator. In Britain, for instance, local party associations play a major part in the enforcement of party regularity in Parliament.[6] It could be that the degree of party voting evident in the United States is also a function of enforcement in the constituency itself or of some other constituency factor. It may also be true, as Froman argues, that differences between Democrats and Republicans "are rooted in basic differences in the kinds of constituencies from which Democrats and Republicans come." [7] In short, the discovery that party is important in legislative behavior may only mask an underlying constituency influence on the legislator.

To know more about politician-constituent relationships, it has become necessary to elaborate upon our original simple model of democracy and to study the various mechanisms that intervene between the people's wishes and the leader's behavior. One of the variables that influence the representation of constituents' wishes is the willingness of the legislator to follow them. Years ago, Edmund Burke told his constituents that a representative should use his own judgment in deciding what will best further the long-range interests of his constituents or of the nation and not just follow his constituents' wishes. Recently a team of scholars discovered that a majority of legislators in four states agree with Burke and assume the role orientation of "trustee" for their constituents. A comparatively small proportion think of themselves as instructed delegates of their constituency, whereas another group seeks to combine the two alternatives into a third, the "politico." [8]

Still other processes intervene between leaders and nonleaders. Lewis Dexter points out that the statement that a congressman "represents" his district is only shorthand for saying that the congressman "represents his image of the district or of his constituents." [9] A full account of representation, therefore, must include representatives' perceptions of their constituents as a variable intervening between the constituents and the behavior of the elected policy-maker. These perceptions may or may not be accurate, but it is necessary to take them into account in order to explain the behavior of the politician.

The image a politician has of his constituents depends in turn upon a complex process of communications between them. Dexter has set forth important generalizations concerning this process.[10] Communications channels from constituents to politicians, for one thing, may exercise an independent effect upon the content of the message that the politicians receive. Information coming from supporters tends to already have a bias—usually a favorable one, because matter unfavorable to the politician is weeded out along the way. Demands of constituents, furthermore, are not necessarily conceived of as "pressure" by the politician, inasmuch as pressure is subjective. Identical communications, therefore, might have very different effects on different politicians.

In addition to the politician's view of his proper role and his image of his constituents, there is a third way in which constituents may exercise a measure of influence on the politician: through the process of recruitment. Regardless of the politician's perceptions or role orientations, constituents may simply select those who agree with them on matters of governmental policy, and turn the representatives who disagree with them out of office. This path of control is explicitly recognized in Miller and Stokes' paradigm of constituency-congressional relations, along with perceptions of the district as another path of constituency influence.[11] With data gathered from both constituents and congressmen, they consider the degree to which constituency attitudes in three public policy areas conformed to congressmen's attitudes on these matters, congressmen's perceptions of constituency attitudes, and congressmen's roll call votes.

To the introduction of processes like role orientation, perception, and recruitment that intervene between the constituency and the politician, we might add another elaboration of the simplest politician-constituent model: a more complex notion of the constituency. A congressman's district is not just "the district" or the majority of rank-and-file voters in that district. Interest-group leaders, party activists, newspaper editors, and others are all important to a politician and are perhaps of more importance than average voters in some circumstances. It is not valid, for example, to say only that because voters possess little information concerning congressmen and because they do not regularly communicate their interest to him, he therefore receives no issue cues and expectations from his constituency, because he may receive a good deal of communication from elements other than rank-and-file voters. Thus, conceiving of the constituency simply as "the district" or as voters alone, hides its complexity. A more complete picture of the constituency would include both voters and elites and also differentiate sharply between the two.

Fortunately, there is a good deal of literature dealing with political elites, particularly with one set of elites that is highly relevant to political electioneering: candidates' supporting coalitions. David Truman's group theory of politics[12] has been followed by some research and theory about the process of building coalitions. William J. Gore and Robert L. Peabody[13] point out that a campaign is a process of welding together a coalition around the candidate. Thus the campaign itself will influence his behavior in office, since the groups that formed his coalition will presumably have access to him throughout his tenure. Major theories of coalition building in diverse contexts have also been constructed. William H. Riker's theory of coalitions[14] makes use of a zero-sum theory of games to predict the size of coalitions. Under the conditions of the model, coalition makers attempt to build minimum winning coalitions, large enough to win the game (for example, the election) but no larger. As the conditions are not met—for example, as uncertainty about the outcome of the election becomes greater—the size of the coalition is altered. The work of Richard M. Cyert and James G. March on business firms,[15] a very different coalition theory, is especially useful here for its treatment of the manner in which decision-makers handle uncertainty. In business firms, uncertainty is avoided by concentrating on short-run decisions and by attempting to control the environment.

The original simple model of democracies, then, has been elaborated in a number of directions. Several intervening mechanisms have been introduced that connect the people and the representative's behavior. A more complex concept of the constituency has also been introduced, one that includes a differentiation between average voters and elites, both important to the politician, together with some propositions about how politicians might build a combination of elites and voters into a supporting coalition.

CONCEPTS

This book, following in the tradition of examining intervening mechanisms, will concentrate on politicians' beliefs about their districts, their sources of information, and the decisions they all must make about which campaign strategies to adopt. Political cognitions such as these are interesting in and of themselves—if only because it is often fascinating simply to discover how people think and doubly fascinating if the people are important figures like politicians—but we deal with these cognitions here because of the direct influence they may have upon the behavior of politicians before and after election to office.

The notion that a person's images of his environment affect his behavior is not new in the social sciences. As one social psychology text states at the beginning of the chapter on cognition, "The social behavior of a person is shaped by the view of the world he has from his particular vantage point." [16] We have already noticed the importance of politicians' perceptions of their constituencies in contemporary treatments of representation. A politician's image of his district may help to explain such matters as his roll call voting, the stands he takes on issues of public policy, and the formulation of his campaign strategies.

A politician's beliefs about his constituents influence

his behavior in at least two ways. First, far from being a passive processor of stimuli, the politician reacts to incoming information before acting upon it. Incoming cues from the constituency are screened and interpreted by the politician. Vital to an explanation of this interpretation is knowledge of his cognitive state before the information was received. Second, politicians are not solely dependent upon specific communications. As many writers have pointed out,[17] the politician not only reacts to incoming cues, but also anticipates the reactions of others to his behavior, including those constituents who might be of importance to him. Examination of the politician's beliefs about his constituents may therefore enable the researcher to construct some propositions about how this anticipation is accomplished.

Several central concepts have guided the research reported in this book. Some have been considered above, but here let us consider them more explicitly. First, rank-and-file voters are vitally important to the politician because a majority of them accept or reject his candidacy at the polls. He is likely, therefore, to consider at least to some degree the effect that his public actions might have on his election chances and, by inference, on voters. Even if average voters are rarely looking over the shoulder of the politician, in other words, it is nevertheless likely that he is looking back over his shoulder at them. So a politician's beliefs about voters constitute an important part of his cognitive map of the district, which in turn influences many of his campaign and policy decisions. Are voters interested in what he is doing? Do election issues have a very great impact? How central is simple party label? What are the attributes of "swing" voters? The conscious or implicit answers that a politician gives to these questions make up his image of voters, a topic considered in Chapter 2.

Average voters, however, are not all there is in a constituency. Various elite groups, because of their numbers, resources, organizational ability, or potential for influencing voters, may also be important to the politician. Among the most important elite groups in terms of election and reelection are the groups in the politician's supporting coalition, for they provide the resources and the effort he needs in order to mount an effective campaign. Because they are important to his chances for election, a politician's beliefs about the members of his supporting coalition are another crucial portion of his image of his district. Who supports him? Why does he think they support him? Does he think they expect anything in return for their support? Who is most important to him in terms of his election chances? Answers to these questions appear in Chapter 3.

A politician, like any other human being, may be viewed as an information-processing organism. His beliefs about his world and his decisions about what to do in response to that world are based in part upon the information that comes to him. Much of the literature surveyed above indicates that reliability of information, the biases evident in many sources, and the ways in which decision-makers assess information sources and deal with the problem of uncertainty about the world are crucial in an explanation of their behavior.[18] Chapter 4 focuses on one kind of important information about the constituency, that related to the politician's election prospects. How certain or uncertain is he about the eventual outcome? What are his sources of information about how he will do, and what reliance does he place on each source? The answers politicians give to these questions allow researchers to investigate the perception and effect of bias in communications, the types of reliability of information, and the ways in which politicians handle whatever uncertainty they might have.

After he has a picture of the voters and the important groups in his constituency, based on whatever information he can muster, the politician's next question must be, "What can I do about it?" Politicians are not simply slates upon which the will of their constituents is written. Rather, they attempt to manipulate their constituency. We will therefore investigate several facets of campaign strategy, which is one kind of behavior affected by the politician's beliefs and his manner of processing information. Why does he choose the issues he does, and how are they presented? Does he make appeals to any particular groups, and if so, who are they and why does he consider them important? Does he concentrate on his strong or his weak areas within the district? These strategic matters are considered in Chapter 5.

In spite of the chapter on campaign strategy, this book is primarily about campaigners, not campaigning. In other words, considerations about politicians' images of their constituencies and their sources of information, although of course relevant to campaigning, are of broader significance. A politician's beliefs about voters, for example, are relevant not only to his choice of campaign strategies but also to the kinds of stands he takes on issues of public policy and to his expression of these stands in his voting in legislative bodies—indeed, to a wide range of his public behavior. The same is true of his beliefs concerning his supporting coalition.

In an attempt to explain differences among politicians, matters of belief and strategy are not only described in this book, but they are also related to a number of other variables. Four of these independent variables are especially important and recur throughout: election outcome, party, type of office sought, and type of district.

Election outcome—whether the politician won or lost and the margin by which he won or lost—might be associated with his beliefs and strategies. This study began with the hypothesis that winners might differ from losers in some systematic way and that this difference could be used to explain some election outcomes. Winners might have more sophisticated notions about the electorate than their opponents and might adopt more effective campaign strategies, or something of the sort; and this fact might help to account for their success. Another hypothesis related to election outcome evolved as the study progressed. This hypothesis, positing a dissonance reduction mechanism,[19] states that losers develop rationalizations for defeat which show up in a number of these beliefs, whereas winners come to congratulate themselves and the district. Thus, election outcome could play a part in structuring the cognitive world of the politician.

Two other variables, incumbency and previous experience in politics, although conceptually distinct from win or loss, are in fact very closely related to election outcome. An extremely small number of the politicians interviewed in this study who *won* in the election, for example, had never before held any offices and few of the incumbent officeholders were defeated. In fact, it is impossible because of prohibitively small cell size to disentangle incumbency and previous experience from election outcome. Partly because of my original interest in possible explanations for wins and losses, I chose to analyze win or loss rather than incumbency or previous political experience.

Political party is the second independent variable. For years, an argument has raged in political science and in popular literature over the extent of party differences in the United States. Proponents of greater party responsibility have sometimes characterized American political parties as Tweedledum and Tweedledee, as organizations with few real, substantial differences. In 1964, the lay counterpart of this feeling was the demand for "a choice, not an echo." Other writers, including many who have done roll call analyses in state and national legislatures, maintain that there are substantial party differences. It could also be that there are greater differences between the parties in individual states than show up in Congress, because of the diffuse nature of American political parties. Party affiliation, in short, seems to be an important explanation for some of the politicians' beliefs and strategies. If Democrats differ from Republicans on the types of coalition members they cite as being important to them, for instance, it would matter a good deal which of the two parties put a man in office.

Whether the politician was running for the state legislature, for the United States Congress, or for a statewide elective office is a third factor that might affect his cognitions. State legislative districts, for one thing, are smaller and are more likely than the larger districts to be socially homogeneous. Those who run for Congress or for a statewide office may also be able to command greater public attention. The whole style of politics in the state legislature might be very different from that in Congress. Therefore, two office levels—the state legislature, on the one hand, and the "higher level" of Congress and statewide elective offices, on the other —are identified and compared.

Finally, the nature of a legislative district or other political unit, generally conceptualized along an urban-rural continuum, has had a long history of use as a research tool by the political scientist. In voting-behavior studies, for example, urban-rural differences in degree of political involvement and strength of party identification have been discovered.[20] In Leon D. Epstein's study of Wisconsin,[21] the rural-urban distinction appears throughout. In this study we will use the area of Wisconsin in which the politician ran—the relatively densely populated southeast portion (including Milwaukee

County), or the more sparsely populated central and
northwest section—rather than the conventional district-
by-district measure of population density.[22] This method
seemed the best to follow because there had been a re-
apportionment just before the interviews were taken,
and past data, including voting history and demographic
information, were not relevant to the new districts. The-
oretically, of course, area of the state may be an important political variable in its own right. One area may
be more prosperous and cosmopolitan than another—
even aside from urban-rural differences—or one may be
exclusively blanketed by the same mass media while
another has a different set of broadcasting stations and
newspapers.

DATA

This book is based on data gathered by personal
interviews with politicians in Wisconsin. These politicians were candidates for a wide variety of offices:
United States senator and congressman, governor, other
statewide elective offices, and the state legislature. I
talked to winners and losers, to members of both parties,
to candidates scattered throughout the state. They were
all people who had run in the 1964 election, and I saw
them about five months after the election, when they
would be more at their leisure than they would have
been during the campaign.

Despite the fact that this data base includes only
1964 candidates in Wisconsin, chosen largely because
they were accessible at the right time, I speak in general
terms about candidates for office. Wisconsin in 1964
was of course unique in some respects. Wisconsin is
well known as the home of the Progressive movement,
with all the traditions and governmental reforms (such
as the direct primary) associated with it. The year 1964
may also have been somewhat unusual—as is any year
—because of Barry Goldwater's Presidential candidacy.

I believe it important, however, to state the propositions developed in this study as generalizations about political behavior, and to invite the replication and testing of these propositions in other contexts.

Readers desiring a more detailed account of the methodology of the study are urged to turn to Appendix A for information concerning the sample design, the interview schedule, and other pertinent methodological details.

NOTES

1. Henry B. Mayo, *An Introduction to Democratic Theory* (New York: Oxford University Press, 1960).

2. Paul F. Lazarsfeld, Bernard R. Berelson, and Hazel Gaudet, *The People's Choice* (New York: Duell, Sloan and Pearce, 1944); Bernard R. Berelson, Paul F. Lazarsfeld, and William N. McPhee, *Voting: A Study of Opinion Formation in a Presidential Campaign* (Chicago: University of Chicago Press, 1954).

3. V. O. Key, Jr., *Public Opinion and American Democracy* (New York: Knopf, 1961).

4. Angus Campbell, Gerald Gurin, and Warren E. Miller, *The Voter Decides* (New York: Harper & Row, 1954); Angus Campbell, Philip E. Converse, Warren E. Miller, and Donald E. Stokes, *The American Voter* (New York: Wiley, 1960).

5. Julius Turner, *Party and Constituency: Pressure on Congress* (Baltimore: Johns Hopkins University Press, 1951); David E. Truman, *The Congressional Party* (New York: Wiley, 1959); Duncan MacRae, Jr., *Dimensions of Congressional Voting* (Berkeley: University of California Press, 1958); Lewis A. Froman, Jr., *Congressmen and Their Constituencies* (Chicago: Rand McNally, 1963).

6. See Austin Ranney, *Pathways to Parliament* (Madison: University of Wisconsin Press, 1965). See also Leon D. Epstein, *British Politics in the Suez Crisis* (Urbana: University of Illinois Press, 1964).

7. Froman, *op. cit.*, p. 89.

8. John C. Wahlke, Heinz Eulau, William Buchanan, and Leroy C. Ferguson, *The Legislative System* (New York: Wiley, 1962), chap. 12.

9. Lewis A. Dexter, "The Representative and His District," *Human Organization*, 16 (1957), 2–13.

10. *Ibid.;* Lewis A. Dexter, "What Do Congressmen Hear: The Mail," *Public Opinion Quarterly*, 20 (1956), 16–27. See also the recent study by Raymond A. Bauer, Ithiel de Sola Pool, and Lewis A. Dexter, *American Business and Public Policy* (New York: Atherton, 1964).

11. Warren E. Miller and Donald E. Stokes, "Constituency Influence in Congress," *American Political Science Review*, 57 (1963), 45–56; "Party Government and the Saliency of Congress," *Public Opinion Quarterly*, 26 (1962), 531–546; see also their forthcoming book; *Representation in the American Congress*.

12. David B. Truman, *The Governmental Process* (New York: Knopf, 1951).

13. William J. Gore and Robert L. Peabody, "The Functions of the Political Campaign: A Case Study," *Western Political Quarterly*, 11 (1958), 55–70.

14. William H. Riker, *The Theory of Political Coalitions* (New Haven: Yale University Press, 1962).

15. Richard M. Cyert and James G. March, *A Behavioral Theory of the Firm* (Englewood Cliffs, N.J.: Prentice-Hall, 1963).

16. David Krech, Richard S. Crutchfield, and Egerton L. Ballachey, *Individual in Society* (New York: McGraw-Hill, 1962), p. 17.

17. See Carl J. Friedrich, *Constitutional Government and Democracy* (Boston: Ginn, 1950), p. 49; and Robert A. Dahl, *Preface to Democratic Theory* (Chicago: University of Chicago Press, 1956), p. 132.

18. See, for example, the works of Dexter (note 10) and of Cyert and March (note 15).

19. For a general statement of the theory upon which this hypothesis is based, see Leon Festinger, *A Theory of Cognitive Dissonance* (New York: Harper & Row, 1957).

20. Campbell, *et al.*, *The American Voter*, *op. cit.*

21. Leon D. Epstein, *Politics in Wisconsin* (Madison: University of Wisconsin Press, 1958).

22. The specific division is by the strata used in the sampling. Milwaukee County and the southeast corner make up the more densely populated area of the state, and Fox Valley, central Wisconsin, and the northwest make up the less densely populated area of the state. See Appendix A.

Chapter 2

BELIEFS
ABOUT VOTERS

★

Knowledge of the politician's beliefs about his district contributes much to our understanding of democratic systems. His image of his constituency may constitute part of the explanation for various important types of behavior, such as his roll call voting, the stands he takes on issues of public policy, and the formulation of his campaign strategies.

A portion of this image is composed of the politician's beliefs about voters—his explicit or implicit theory of voting behavior. Because holding office is contingent upon the approval of a majority of voters in an election, he is likely to consider at least to some degree the effect his various decisions might have on election outcomes. In making such judgments, the politician probably makes some assumptions, conscious or not, about the manner in which voters choose among candidates. If he believes, for example, that voters pay close attention to his actions, he probably feels more constrained by his district's likely opinions than if he does not hold that belief.[1] Thus, his beliefs about voters may be an important part of his image of his district, and in turn may affect his decisions on crucial roll calls, policy stands, campaigns, and the like.

Politicians' beliefs about voters have been considered important for another reason: they may account for the campaign strategies candidates adopt and perhaps for the success of these strategies in winning votes. Austin Ranney and Willmoore Kendall maintain that politicians base their campaigns on "reflective analysis of past experience, i.e., theory," their theory of how to win votes.[2] Comments after each election suggest that the successful candidate in the election had a theory of voting behavior different from that held by the loser. The unsuccessful candidate, the argument runs, lost because he made several crucial mistakes, many of them involving his judgments about voters. By some accounts, for example, Adlai Stevenson overestimated the degree to which voters were interested in the issues he was discussing. The study of the 1964 election by Philip E. Converse, Aage R. Clausen, and Warren E. Miller states that Barry Goldwater's campaign "assumed an electorate with near-total ideological comprehension and sensitivity," that his actions were based on "a sort of chronic miscalculation of electoral reality." [3]

A comparison of winners' and losers' beliefs about voters, therefore, might prove fruitful in terms of explaining campaign strategy and even some election outcomes. We will first examine differences between the beliefs of winning and losing candidates, then consider alternative explanations for the results and suggest some possible theoretical implications of the findings.

THE BELIEFS

In this research, the politicians were asked questions about voters patterned after conclusions from survey research studies. These studies have discovered that a relatively small proportion of voters is highly interested in and informed about politics, so respondents were asked to indicate how politically interested and informed they think voters are.[4] The voting studies have also identified a number of variables that influence voters' choices, including relatively static ones which are stable over a long period of time, like party identification, and relatively dynamic ones which change from election to election, like the voters' attitudes toward the candidates and the issues of a particular election. Questions concerning these variables were structured according to the analysis in *The Voter Decides,* in which the authors identify three variables that heavily influence voters' choices: party identification, issue partisanship, and candidate orientation. Respondents were therefore asked to assess the importance of party, issues, and candidates.[5]

Winners' and losers' ratings of the importance of these three variables on voters' decisions appear in Table 2-1. Both winners and losers downgrade issues and upgrade candidates' personal characteristics, in what is perhaps eloquent testimony to a general tendency of human beings to believe that the world in which they live revolves around themselves. The unsuccessful candidates, however, give great emphasis to the importance of party label and decidedly downgrade the importance of issues as determinants of voters' choices. One unsuccessful candidate complained, "Look at the last election. Nobody listened to the issues," and another said, "The issues aren't much good in an area where people have made up their minds ten years in advance." Winners, on the other hand, while splitting

TABLE 2-1

**Comparison of Winners and Losers on Importance
Attached to Party, Issues, Candidates***

Importance	Party		Issues		Candidates	
	WIN-NERS	LOS-ERS	WIN-NERS	LOS-ERS	WIN-NERS	LOS-ERS
All or very important	44%	80%	42%	27%	84%	63%
Some, little, or no importance	56	20	58	73	16	37
	100%	100%	100%	100%	100%	100%
n	32	30	31	30	32	30

* Respondents were handed a card with party identification, issue orientation, and candidate orientation stated in layman's language at the top: "Party label, issues of the election, personal characteristics of the candidates." The following evaluational categories were at the bottom: "All important, very important, of some importance, of little importance, not important." Respondents were then asked the following question: "Consider the three factors at the top of this card. Would you tell me how important each of these is in determining the choice of the voters? You can use the categories at the bottom of the card."

roughly equally on party label and issues, tend to believe that their own personal characteristics are important influences on voters' behavior.

To characterize what may be their patterns of thought, the winners tend to believe more than the losers that the voters in their district decided how to cast their ballots not by blind party voting but according to the issues of the election and the man who was seeking the office. They tend more than the losers to congratulate the electorate for deciding on the "right" bases because, after all, the electorate made the right choice. Relative to winners, however, unsuccessful candidates blame the electorate for their loss by emphasizing the importance of the party label and by downgrading the importance of issues and the candidates. They deprecate the electorate's decision because, after all, it was not the wise decision.

The same conclusion emerges from the respondents' rank-ordering of party label, issues of the election, and personal characteristics of the candidates. Table 2-2

TABLE 2-2

Comparison of Winners and Losers on Rank Assigned to Party Label, Issues, Candidates' Characteristics*

Variable	Most Important		Least Important	
	WINNERS	LOSERS	WINNERS	LOSERS
Party label	21%	59%	47%	17%
Election issues	17	7	50	55
Characteristics of candidates	62	35	3	28
	100%	101%†	100%	100%
n	29	29	30	29

* The response card outlined in the note to Table 2-1 was again used. The question used was: "If you were to rank the three factors, which would you say is most important in determining the choice voters will make? Which is second?"
† Rounding error.

shows how many winners and losers ranked each of the three factors as first in importance and how many ranked each of them as least important. Again, winners tend to place great emphasis on their own personal characteristics as determinants of voters' decisions and to assign party label a relatively low place. By comparison, losers tend to upgrade party label and downgrade the personal characteristics of the candidates.

Although both groups tend to place little emphasis on issues, winners tend more than losers to congratulate the electorate for "voting for the man," and losers tend more than winners to blame the electorate for "blindly voting for party labels."

A breakdown of the responses of successful candidates indicates that the congratulation effect shown in the figures on the importance of party and issues in Table 2-1 and the "least important" ranking in Table 2-2 is actually due to the beliefs of the marginal winners, those who won by under 55 percent of the two-party vote. Whereas "safe" winners tend to stress the importance of party label and downgrade the importance of issues in approximately the same proportions as both marginal and decisive losers, two-thirds of the marginal winners think that issues are all or very important and that party label ranks last in importance. Some 80 percent of the marginal winners rate party label as of some, little, or no importance. Regardless of the decisiveness of the win or loss, however, both types of winners still tend to rate the personal characteristics of the candidates as more important than losers do (Table 2-1). All winners also tend to rank personal characteristics of the candidates as the most important of the three variables, whereas losers rank party label as the most important (Table 2-2). These differences between marginal and decisive winners are accentuated in the case of successful candidates for the state legislature.

It seems evident that marginal winners in some instances are making judgments not about the motivations of voters in general but rather about the sorts of variables that are thought to influence votes at the margin where they are of crucial importance. Because their districts tend to be evenly balanced between the parties, issues are thought to be of great importance and party identification of less importance because it has less effect on "swing" votes in the middle. The safe winners, on the other hand—probably because their districts obviously favor one party or the other—emphasize the importance of party label.

The candidates interviewed also stated how interested in their campaigns and how informed about the issues of the election they thought voters were. A comparison of the responses of successful and unsuccessful candidates[6] appears in Table 2-3. The cross-tabulation

TABLE 2-3

Comparison of Winners' and Losers' Beliefs about Degree of Voter Interest and Information*

| Degree | Interested | | Informed | |
	WINNERS	LOSERS	WINNERS	LOSERS
Very	32%	43%	26%	3%
Some	42	20	42	27
None	26	37	32	70
	100%	100%	100%	100%
n	31	30	31	30

* The question: "Generally speaking, would you say that voters in your district are interested in your campaign, or not?" If the respondent said they were interested: "Would you say they're *very* interested?" About information: "Do you think that voters in your district are informed about the way the candidates stand on the issues of the election, or not?" If informed: "Are they *very* well informed?"

on information clearly shows another case of the congratulation-rationalization effect. Losers are inclined very strongly to believe that voters are not informed about the issues of the election. One unsuccessful candidate remarked, "I had relations vote against me because they didn't know it was me running." Winners tend to believe that voters are much better informed. One successful candidate thought voters were somewhat informed: "Oh, not to the point of being technically informed. They are generally aware of my overall record, and if I have slipped up, they know it." A full quarter of the winners (most of them safe winners) even think that voters are very well informed about the issues. Differences of opinion on how well voters are informed are especially pronounced at the statewide and federal levels.

The picture in the case of voters' interest in the campaign is less clear. Winners tend to believe that voters are somewhat interested in their campaigns, as this congressman observed: "A little interested, but not highly interested. Most are likely to know who the congressman is, and a couple of major things about him." Losers tend to believe that voters either are not interested or are very interested. Most of those losers who believe that voters are very interested in their campaigns have never held any public elective office. This finding may be due to the tendency on the part of some inexperienced unsuccessful candidates, particularly candidates for the state legislature, to believe that they did accomplish at least one thing—they got people interested—and they at least feel the satisfaction of having aroused the electorate. It is likely that many politicians would not care to feel that their strenuous effort during a campaign had absolutely no effect on voters. A minimum justification for the many hours and dollars poured into campaigning would be that the campaign at least stimulated interest.

There are some close relationships among these various beliefs about voters, indicating some degree of cognitive consistency on the part of these politicians. First, ratings of the importance of each of the three variables—party, issues, and candidates—are closely associated with respondents' rank-ordering of the three, as one would expect. Second, perceived voter interest and perceived voter information are closely related, with election outcome (win or loss) controlled. Those candidates who have a high estimate of voter information also tend to believe that voters are interested in the campaign, and vice versa. Assessments of voter interest and information are also related to perceived importance of the election issues, with election outcome controlled. This relationship, though not strong, is consistent and suggests that those who have a low estimate of voter interest and information also have a low estimate of the importance of the election issues. For instance, half of the winners who believe that voters are "very well informed" also believe that issues are "very important," but less than a quarter of the winners who believe that voters are not informed also believe that issues are very important. Similarly, over half of the winners who believe that voters are "very interested" in the campaign believe that issues are also very important, but a quarter of those who believe that voters are not interested also believe that issues are very important.

Taken together, these findings suggest some degree of cognitive consistency among politicians' beliefs about voters. There is apparently a general tendency to praise the voters: to estimate high levels of interest, information, and issue awareness among voters, quite apart from the effect that winning or losing has on the candidate's beliefs.[7] Other candidates, however, have a general tendency to deprecate the voters' interest, information, and issue awareness—again apart from whether they won or lost. Although the sample is small and the relationships are not overly strong, the consistency of the result from one cross-tabulation to another leads to the conclusion that there is some degree of consistency among the beliefs about voters.

The congratulation-rationalization effect cited earlier can be discerned *within* politicians as well as between winners and losers, making the effect intra-individual as well as inter-individual. Respondents were asked to summarize the major factors that had led to their political victories and defeats over the years. As Table 2-4 shows, respondents strongly attributed their wins to

TABLE 2-4

Respondents' Beliefs About Major Factors Contributing to Wins and Defeats*

FACTORS	WINS	DEFEATS
Beyond R's control	25%	91%
Within R's control	75	9
	100%	100%
n	40†	44†

* The question was: "Could you summarize the major factors that have contributed to your wins and defeats over the years?"

† The total number is lower than the sample size of 62 because many respondents either had never won or had never lost.

factors under their own control: hard work, personal service to constituents, campaign strategy, building a reputation, and better publicity. Respondents very often attributed losses, on the other hand, to factors beyond their control, such as the party make-up of the district, the familiar name or other unbeatable characteristics of their opponent, national and state trends, and lack of money. It was a comparatively rare respondent who attributed his win to his good political name, for instance, or to the predominance of his party in his district; and respondents very rarely attributed their defeats to laziness, failure to serve constituents, mistakes in campaign strategy, or similar causes.

It is possible that the type of office sought by the candidate might be relevant—that those who ran for the state legislature might have different beliefs about voters from those who ran for higher-level offices. The results of this study show that type of office sought seemed to

have no substantial effect on the congratulation-rationalization effect. Winners differed from losers at both
levels in the manner already described. But when the
winners at the higher level are compared to the winners
at the state legislative level and the losers at the two
levels are also compared, some differences between the
two levels emerge. In general, party label is believed to
be more important and issues less important at the state
legislative level than at the higher level.[8] Also, winners
at the higher level believe that voters are more politically
interested and informed than do winners at the legislative level.[9]

There was one matter upon which most candidates
agreed. Two-thirds of the respondents felt that party
voters were more interested and informed than independents. Some respondents spoke of "party identifiers,"
agreeing with the politician who said:

> If a person feels deeply, he'll get into a party. There
> are very few dispassionate political observers, unless
> you're a political scientist or something. We're emo-
> tional creatures, and it's hard to really be interested
> and not get involved.

Others criticized independents for hiding their lack of
interest behind a façade of considered judgment. "Those
who are lazy and not interested can say they're independents," one candidate said, and another remarked,
"When you talk to these independents and ask them
about this and that, you draw a blank, and then he
comes out with this, 'I vote for the man.' "

There is some hint in these and other responses of
a distinctive frame of reference employed by many
politicians within which they form their beliefs about
voters. Among the politicians interviewed, there was a
widespread tendency to classify people into two categories: the independent voter and the party *activist*.
Many respondents would not talk about a party *voter*,

even though the question called for it. This tendency to interpret voter phenomena in the light of various sorts of elite behavior occurs in other contexts. Many respondents, for example, judged voter interest in the campaign by reference to various phenomena at the elite level, such as the number of people who volunteer to campaign. Even when asked directly about them, some politicians treat rank-and-file voters as a comparatively unknown realm and interpret statements concerning them in the light of phenomena closer to themselves: the elite, mass media, party activists. Though the evidence on this point is tenuous, the hypothesis that to a great extent, politicians operate in an elite cognitive world, largely isolated from rank-and-file voters, may account for some of these findings.

EXPLANATIONS

Analysis of the survey responses indicates that winning and losing candidates have divergent beliefs about the behavior of voters—winners believe voters to be better informed, more issue- and candidate-oriented, and less party-oriented than losers do. In competitive districts, these differences between winners and losers are especially pronounced.

The findings have been explained in terms of a "congratulation-rationalization effect." To state this explanation more fully here, I have maintained that winners develop complimentary beliefs about voters and losers develop rationalizations for their losses simply by virtue of the outcome of the election. Winners, the argument runs, believe that the voters did a good job of choosing. Voters in their view are well informed about politics and vote according to the issues and the candidates, rather than blindly following their party. Losers, on the other hand, rationalize defeat by saying that voters are ill-informed and vote according to party label rather than the issues or the men who are running for office. Both winners and losers, in other words, re-arrange their cognitions about voters to take account of the outcome of the election: winners congratulate the voters, and losers rationalize their defeat. This sort of reaction might be expected to occur to some extent even before election day, since some candidates probably anticipate the outcome. This congratulation-rationalization effect can be conceived as a mechanism for reducing the cognitive dissonance between beliefs about voters and election outcome.[10]

Alternative explanations for the findings are available. The belief that voters are interested in and informed about politics and vote on the basis of the issues of the election, for example, is probably a socially acceptable belief in the American culture. Incumbent officeholders may therefore feel somewhat obliged to hold the "correct" beliefs, whereas losers, because they may not confront the prospect of facing the voters in subsequent elections, may not feel similarly bound. Such an explanation does not simply dismiss the findings as conscious distortions of the incumbents' beliefs for the benefit of the interviewer. This sort of conscious deception seems unlikely, because respondents were assured of their anonymity and the questions were not particularly sensitive. This alternative explanation, rather, maintains that unsuccessful candidates have in a sense been rejected by their society and therefore no longer feel obliged to give the socially acceptable response.

Another alternative may be labeled the "incumbency" explanation. Incumbent officeholders, after all, live in a highly politicized world. They regularly deal with people involved in at least some aspects of government, and they may think of themselves as the center of attention. They simply extend these experiences with elite citizens to their conceptions of the voters at large. Many respondents cited such nonvoter elements as letters received, enthusiasm of campaign workers, contributions, and the number of bumper stickers as evidence of rank-and-file voter interest. Even when the interviewer attempted to probe back to a consideration of average voters, many respondents continued to confuse the behavior of political elites with that of voters. Because everyone with whom incumbents come in contact is involved in the affairs of government, they may come to assume that this is the natural state of affairs with all voters.

Another possible result of incumbency is a tendency to concentrate on those determinants of voting behavior that can be manipulated by the politician. It may be that marginal winners in this study rated the dynamic variables of issue and candidate as particularly important not because they believed these factors influence voters more than party identification does, but because issues and candidates change from election to election and therefore are capable of being manipulated by the politician more than are stable party loyalties. Marginal winners, furthermore, because party loyalties are evenly balanced in their districts, may rate party as "not important" in the sense that it cannot account for shifts from election to election, which are of vital interest to them. As one Republican winner said, "If the district went Democratic last time, the party couldn't be too important, could it?" Thus, another possible explanation for some of the findings may be that marginal winners, far from being "unrealistic" in an absolute sense, instead choose the "reality" that is most relevant to their own election and reelection. Marginal losers, on the other hand, now freed from such a concern and perhaps personally threatened by the possibility that they lost because their issue positions or personal characteristics were unacceptable to the majority of the electorate, rationalize their defeat by asserting the importance of party label. There may be more rationalization than congratulation.

It is difficult to state conclusively which combination of explanations accounts for the responses received. There is one further piece of evidence that remains to be considered; it will be discussed in the following section along with some speculations about the political consequences of the beliefs we have found politicians to hold.

IMPLICATIONS

Election Success. One explanation for at least some election outcomes, set forth at the beginning of this chapter, is that the winning candidate based his campaign on a more accurate perception of voting behavior than the loser did. Although preelection interviews were not conducted for this study, there are certain inferences that we may draw concerning beliefs of politicians before the election.

Considering first only the postelection interview data, it would be difficult to maintain that winners have more accurate beliefs about voting behavior than losers do, once election day is past. Survey research studies of voting behavior have discovered, generally speaking, that a rather small proportion of the electorate is highly interested in and informed about politics, even in Presidential elections.[11] Voter awareness and involvement seems even more minimal in the case of congressional elections, in which voters' images of the candidates and their knowledge of the election issues are considerably weaker.[12] Both Presidential and congressional campaigns are probably more salient than are contests for the state legislature.[13] Against this backdrop of evidence about the actual degree of voter involvement, it seems clear that (at least after the election) successful candidates tend to overestimate the degree to which voters are interested in politics, informed about governmental matters, and conscious of election issues.

The relative importance of party, issues, and candidates as perceived by politicians is more difficult to analyze. In this case, it appears that both winners and losers select a version of "reality" consonant with their particular postelection situation. Winners tend to emphasize the dynamic, manipulable variables that affect votes at the margin, whereas losers tend to emphasize party label. Both of these responses could conceivably be considered "realistic," depending on the frame of reference evoked by the analyst. Especially in view of the data on the respondents' beliefs about the degree of political interest and information in the electorate, however, it would still be difficult to maintain that after the election, the winners have *more* accurate beliefs about the voters than the losers do.

The preelection beliefs of these respondents may have been different from the postelection beliefs obtained for this study. One possibility is that potential winners' and losers' beliefs about voters were actually quite similar and that congratulation and especially rationalization occurred after the election. Alternatively, those who were to be winners may even then have had a higher estimate of voter political involvement than those who were to be losers simply because both correctly anticipated the outcome to some extent, even though the differences between them would be greater after election day. The hypothesis of greater perceptual accuracy on the part of winners, however, would require that preelection potential winners have a lower estimate of voter interest, information, and issue- and candidate-awareness than those who subsequently became losers. There seems to be little reason to expect such a preelection configuration, for it is precisely the reverse of the postelection case. Therefore, although the data presented here are not measurements of the candidates' preelection beliefs, they nevertheless suggest that it is difficult to account for election success in terms of the winning candidate's more accurate perception of voting behavior.

These statements do not imply that successful candidates conduct less effective campaigns than unsuccessful candidates do or that winners succeed in spite of their campaigns rather than because of them. This conclusion would assume that campaigns are oriented toward voters, an assumption that may not hold in fact. It could be, indeed, that political campaigning is carried on according to considerations relatively far removed from voters, such as the requirements of the media, the timing of the campaign, the actions of one's opponent, and the demands of such nonmass, elite elements as party activists, campaign contributors, and interest-group leaders. A successful candidate may base his campaign largely on these nonvoter variables and still conduct a campaign that is effective in winning votes. We might speculate, however, that whatever campaign strategies may account for election success, these strategies do not appear to be based on beliefs about voters that correspond to the conclusions about voter involvement drawn from survey research studies of voting behavior.

There is one other piece of evidence that bears on this question. Both before and after the 1966 election, William Stewart[14] mailed identical questionnaires to candidates for the lower house of the Michigan state legislature, asking them to rank-order party, issues, and candidates and to estimate the degree of interest and information in the electorate. The wording of the questions was patterned after the wording of the questionnaire for the Wisconsin study. The methodological problems in a mail questionnaire are legion, including possible different standards of interpretation by respondents, overstructuring of the questions, lack of rapport with respondents, and low rate of return. Evidence from this source, therefore, must be taken as only suggestive.

The Michigan data show substantial rationalization on the part of the losing candidates with regard to the relative importance of party, issues, and candidates. Before the election, 36 percent of the subsequent losers ranked issues of the election as the least important of the three, but after the election, 77 percent of the losers did so. Similarly, before the election, 56 percent of the subsequent losers ranked party label as most important of the three, whereas the postelection figure for losers was 86 percent. Winners, on the other hand, exhibit few consistent shifts between the periods before and after the election, aside from a slight tendency to rank candidates more important and issues less important after the election than they did before. As for their beliefs about the degree of political interest and information in the electorate, few consistent differences between pre- and postelection responses emerged, except for some tendency on the part of winners to reply in greater numbers after the election than before that voters are very interested in the campaign.

The mail questionnaire shows the same differences between winners and losers that the Wisconsin study reports. Winners have a higher estimate of voter interest and information than losers. Losers tend to rank party label as most important, and winners rank the personal characteristics of the candidate as most important. These comparisons between winners and losers apply both before and after the election. Even before election day, for instance, 23 percent of the subsequent winners say that voters are very well informed about the issues of the election, but only 3 percent of the subsequent losers do. These considerable differences between winners and losers even before the election probably indicate that to some degree the politicians are anticipating the outcome and at least subconsciously taking the likely result into account. In fact, when respondents were asked directly whether they "really expect to win," all of those who subsequently won indicated that they did expect to win; but 64 percent of the subsequent losers expected to win, indicating that this anticipation of the outcome does occur to an extent.

Results from such a short mail questionnaire cannot be regarded as definitive. Apparently, however, winners did not have preelection beliefs about voters that corresponded to the findings of survey research studies of voting behavior to a greater degree than did those of subsequent losers. In fact, if anything, the subsequent losers' beliefs conform more closely to the survey findings. There appears to be some congratulation on the part of the winners and a good deal of rationalization on the part of the losers, both in direct response to the election returns themselves and in anticipation of the final outcome. Of course, the possible effects of incumbency discussed earlier may partially account for these preelection findings.

State-National Differences. We have discovered that candidates for the state legislature tend to believe that voters are less interested in their races, less informed about the issues, and more party-oriented than do candidates for statewide offices or Congress. This felt isolation from voters on the part of state legislative candidates may have several important political consequences. First, if state legislators believe that voters in their districts are highly party-oriented, this belief may influence the high degree of party cohesion found in many state legislatures.[15] Election success in these states might be considered a function of standing with the party, but members of Congress might not feel similarly indebted to their party.

It has also been maintained that interest-group activity on the state level is quite different from that on the national level. Several of Lester W. Milbrath's respondents, for example, think lobbying is "cleaner" in Washington than in their state capitols.[16] Perhaps one restraint on interest-group activity is voter involvement in politics as perceived by legislators. According to Ralph K. Huitt, for example, one of Senator William Proxmire's beliefs about politics is that a "strong hold on the electorate, which can control [the legislator] only in the most general sense, enables him to resist any group (including his staunch supporters) which might seek to exercise specific influence." [17] Our data, then, suggest that state legislators and members of Congress differ in the degree to which they think that voters are involved in their campaigns. This difference might partially explain the amount of interest-group activity at the two levels. Other differences between state legislative and higher-level politicians, reported in subsequent chapters, bolster this speculation.

It appears, then, that politicians' theories of voting behavior may be related to the whole style of politics found in different political systems. More research that systematically compares similar phenomena at state and national levels is needed, however, before any definitive conclusions can be reached.

Communications. Let us return to the broad problem of communication between representative and constituents that is a major focus of this study. Raymond A. Bauer, Ithiel de Sola Pool, and Lewis Anthony Dexter state that even in the case of relations with his constituents, who have the powerful sanction of reelection at their disposal, "the congressman is quite free" within the limits of "what is morally or sociologically conceivable." [18] My research suggests that the representative's freedom may vary according to his theory of voting behavior, that the representative who believes that voters pay attention to election issues probably is less free of his constituents than one who does not.[19]

To elaborate, the rearrangement of a politician's cognitions by virtue of his election may have important implications for his behavior while in office. The incumbent is more likely than if he lost to believe that voters are watching him, that they are well informed, and that they made their choice according to the candidates' personal characteristics or even according to the issues of the election. Because of these results of electoral victory, the incumbent may be easier to influence than if there were no congratulation-rationalization effect. He might pay greater attention to his constituency because he believes that his constituents are paying greater attention to him than he might think if he had lost. Winners differ from one another as well, of course, in their estimate of voter political involvement—and hence in the degree to which the district is likely to influence them.

Constituency influence on an officeholder need not depend on the reception of direct cues from the district. The politician acts not only according to cues, such as mail, that reach him directly from his constituents, but also according to his conception of their probable reaction to the various alternatives he might choose. This notion that incumbents anticipate the reactions of people who are important to them, particularly the electorate in the case of elective officials, is common to a number of writers in political science and has been set forth by Carl J. Friedrich as the "rule of anticipated reactions." [20] The importance of these anticipated reactions is probably heightened by the congratulation-rationalization effect. By virtue of his electoral victory, an officeholder (especially a marginal winner) believes that the eyes of the public are on him, that voters cast their ballots according to his actions and characteristics, and that they are comparatively well informed about the issues of an election. If an incumbent thinks the electorate is watching him, whether they are or not in fact, he will attempt to anticipate their reactions to his decisions. In this way, the congratulation-rationalization effect may increase the influence a constituency has on an officeholder.

NOTES

1. See Warren E. Miller and Donald E. Stokes, "Constituency Influence in Congress," *American Political Science Review,* 57 (1963), 45–56. A secondary analysis of the Miller and Stokes data collected by the University of Michigan Survey Research Center does suggest, in fact, that congressmen with a high estimate of voter awareness vote with their district's views more than those with a low estimate. See John W. Kingdon, "Politicians' Beliefs about Voters," *American Political Science Review,* 61 (1967), 137.

2. Austin Ranney and Willmoore Kendall, *Democracy and the American Party System* (New York: Harcourt, Brace & World, 1956), pp. 340–44.

3. Philip E. Converse, Aage R. Clausen, and Warren E. Miller, "Electoral Myth and Reality: The 1964 Election," *American Political Science Review,* 59 (1965), 332, 335.

4. The exact phrasing of questions appears in footnotes to the tables.

5. For the survey studies on these points, see Angus Campbell, Gerald Gurin, and Warren E. Miller, *The Voter Decides* (New York: Harper & Row, 1954); Angus Campbell, Philip E. Converse, Warren E. Miller, and Donald E. Stokes, *The American Voter* (New York: Wiley, 1960); and Angus Campbell and Donald E. Stokes, "Partisan Attitudes and the Presidential Vote," in Eugene Burdick and Arthur J. Brodbeck (eds.), *American Voting Behavior* (New York: Free Press, 1959).

6. The decisiveness of the win or loss has no substantial impact on these results, except where noted.

7. Election outcome was controlled. That is, data that could show the relationship between perceived interest and

perceived issue importance, for example, was tabulated separately for winners and for losers, and each relationship examined.

8. The proportion of state legislative winners saying that party label is all or very important is 56 percent; the proportion of higher-level winners saying the same is 31 percent. The proportions of winners saying that issues are all or very important are legislative, 33 percent; higher-level, 50 percent.

9. Of the state legislative winners, 13 percent say that voters are very interested in their campaigns, and 50 percent of the higher-level winners say so. The proportion of state legislative winners saying that voters are very well informed is 13 percent; of higher-level winners, 38 percent.

10. For the general theory upon which this statement is based, see Leon Festinger, *A Theory of Cognitive Dissonance* (New York: Harper & Row, 1957).

11. Campbell, *et al.*, *The American Voter, op. cit.*

12. Miller and Stokes, *op. cit.*

13. See Herbert Jacob and Kenneth N. Vines (eds.), *Politics in the American States* (Boston: Little, Brown, 1965), p. 29.

14. Stewart, a University of Michigan student, sent the preelection questionnaire to a systematic sample of 110 candidates opposed to each other in the general election. After one follow-up reminder, he obtained a 75 percent rate of return. The postelection questionnaire was sent only to those who responded to the preelection query, and of these, 65 percent responded. Overall, therefore, about half the candidates originally contacted responded to both questionnaires, a sample of 53. I wish to thank him for the use of these data.

15. Jacob and Vines, *op. cit.*, p. 88.

16. Lester W. Milbrath, *The Washington Lobbyists* (Chicago: Rand McNally, 1963), pp. 301–04.

17. Ralph K. Huitt, "The Outsider in the Senate: An Alternative Role," *American Political Science Review,* 55 (1961), 568.

18. Raymond A. Bauer, Ithiel de Sola Pool, and Lewis Anthony Dexter, *American Business and Public Policy* (New York: Atherton, 1964), p. 423.

19. Additional evidence for the proposition is presented in Kingdon, *op. cit.*

20. Carl J. Friedrich, *Constitutional Government and Democracy* (Boston: Ginn, 1950), p. 49. Other writers have also used essentially the same concept. These include V. O. Key, Jr., *Public Opinion and American Democracy* (New York: Knopf, 1961), p. 263, "latency of public opinion"; David B. Truman, *The Governmental Process* (New York: Knopf, 1951), p. 34, "potential groups"; and Robert A. Dahl, *Preface to Democratic Theory* (Chicago: University of Chicago Press, 1956), p. 132.

Chapter 3

COALITIONS

Rank-and-file voters are not the sum of a constituency. A candidate for office also receives cues and perceives expectations from political elites in the district, including party activists, interest-group leaders, newspaper editors, and his own campaign volunteers. Indeed, these elite groups may be of far more immediate consequence to the politician than considerations about rank-and-file voters. One of the reasons for the considerable amount of dissonance reduction evident in the candidates' beliefs about voters, for example, may be that voters constitute a relatively distant realm, and it is considerably easier to distort the motivations, attitudes, and behavior of others in a system whose activities are far removed from the actor in question than it is to distort the behavior of those with whom the actor has more direct experience. In a consideration of politicians' cognitions about their constituencies, some attention must therefore be paid to these elites.

Among the elite groups most important to the candidate for office are those that make up his supporting coalition. These groups, after all, provide finances and campaign workers, and, to an extent, contribute their influence with certain voters—all of which help the candidate in his attempt to gain office. This chapter therefore concentrates on the groups that form the politician's supporting coalition, as he sees them.

Coalitions are important not only to the politician seeking office, but also to the political scientist seeking explanations for political behavior. Once a politician gains office, the groups in his supporting coalition will probably have greater access to the decision-maker than will groups opposed to him. It is also likely that the incumbent is to some degree limited in his choice of alternatives by the type of coalition he has gathered around him. A Democrat with a coalition that depends heavily on organized labor, for example, would find it difficult to vote against a series of bills that would benefit labor without endangering his tenure as a legislator. The same would be true for a business-oriented Republican. Furthermore, if it can be shown that the two political parties are generally supported by very different coalitions, then which party gains control of the governmental machinery becomes important.

This study investigates coalitions *only* as they are seen by the candidate. The coalition that affects a politician's behavior is not necessarily identical to the coalition that supports him in fact. It is conceivable, for example, that a candidate for office could depend rather heavily on the support of the business community and at the same time not recognize the extent of his dependence. The extent of the influence of the business members of his coalition would depend, however, on his *beliefs* about the importance of their support for his election chances, rather than its actual extent and importance. It becomes important to ask who the politician believes constitutes his supporting coalition and what the characteristics of these supporting groups are as he sees them.

First, then, we will present politicians' simple accounts of who supported them. Second, we will consider why he believes each group mentioned supported him and whether or not they expected anything of him in return for their support. Third, we will discuss which coalition members were most important to the candidate in terms of his election chances and to which ones, if any, the politician felt he could afford to pay less attention.

COALITION MEMBERS

It has often been said that there is no essential difference between the two major political parties in the United States. Their platforms are similar in most important respects, they embrace such diverse elements that programmatically some Republicans appear to be Democrats and vice versa, their members do not vote together in Congress, and neither presents a coherent, unified face to the American people. The words "Republican" and "Democrat," the argument runs, have little "meaning" in terms of public policy alternatives.

Others argue that there are indeed substantial party differences in the United States. Many roll call studies have found party differences in congressional voting.[1] Blocs do exist within each party, of course, but the simple fact that a congressman is a Republican or a Democrat explains more of his votes than the area from which he comes, the kind of constituency he represents, or other possible determinants of voting. It is therefore evident that there are meaningful programmatic differences between the parties and that these differences are important in studying the legislative process.

In *Congressmen and Their Constituencies*,[2] Lewis A. Froman makes a beginning at explaining differences between the two parties on the basis that the party members represent different types of constituencies. Froman states that constituency characteristics would explain much more of the difference between the two political parties than his analysis of demographic variables permits, if the "congressman's perception of his district and what he considers to be his effective constituency" were taken into account.[3] Republicans and Democrats, in other words, might be representing consistently different sorts of elements within their districts, which could help to account for party differences in congressional roll call votes.

One way to measure this "representation" of different elements is to examine the candidates' perceived supporting coalitions. If the candidates of each party are supported by different coalitions, the two parties can be conceived of as representing different elements within their districts, and the divergent types of coalitions could then be useful in accounting for party differences.

Respondents in the Wisconsin study were asked what groups of people supported their candidacies in the last election. A wide variety of supporting groups was listed: businessmen; labor; professional people such as doctors and lawyers; farmers; and "noneconomic" groups such as lodges, clubs, ethnic groups, and educators. Despite this proliferation of possible supporting coalitions, however, three basic types could be identified. The first—labeled here a "business-oriented" coalition —includes business and professional groups and perhaps several other groups but does not include organized labor. The second includes labor and perhaps several other groups but does not include business and professional groups and is called a "labor-oriented" coalition. The third group of coalitions straddles the labor-business dichotomy. Eight respondents said they had the support of both business and labor, and several others cited a coalition of supporting groups that includes neither. A fourth category of respondents, however, indicated that they had no group support or refused to talk about group support, saying either that group categories were not meaningful or that they preferred not to recognize such categories.

Table 3-1 demonstrates the dramatic party differ-

TABLE 3-1

Parties' Supporting Coalitions

Type of Coalition	Party	
	DEMOCRATS	REPUBLICANS
Labor-oriented	72%	0%
Business-oriented	0	43
Neither: both labor and business, farm, noneconomic	22	30
Refused to discuss groups, no group support	6	27
	100%	100%
n	32	30

ences in supporting coalitions. Democratic candidates for office list an essentially labor-oriented coalition, one that includes labor but not business, and Republicans tend to have a business-oriented coalition. A number of Republicans also refuse to discuss group support (see Chapter 5 for an explanation). Most important here, not a single Democrat in the study listed a coalition that included business and professional groups but not labor, and not a single Republican mentioned a labor-oriented coalition. Table 3-1 contains probably the most striking results reported in this study, and it shows very clearly that there are extreme party differences in terms of supporting groups, as those groups are seen by the candidates. It is important to emphasize that Republicans were characterizing their *own* supporters and that Democrats were listing their own as well.

There are also differences in coalition support between the relatively urban area of the state and the relatively rural area, with party held constant. Only 13 percent of the candidates in the southeast portion of the state, which includes the relatively large cities of Milwaukee, Racine, Kenosha, and Madison, list a coalition that includes both business and labor or includes farmers and noneconomic groups but neither business nor labor, whereas 39 percent of the respondents in the more small-town and rural northwest portion of the state list this kind of coalition. Among Democrats, all except one of the candidates in the southeast enumerate a labor-oriented coalition, but half of the northwest Democrats have a coalition that does not include labor or includes both labor and business at the same time. Republicans from the southeast are also more likely to have a business-oriented coalition than Republicans from the northwest. The labor-business dichotomy, therefore, is more in evidence in the more urban parts of the state than in the relatively small-town and rural areas.

To this point in the discussion, we have conceived of the politician's supporting coalition largely as a collection of political interest groups. Respondents who cited supporting groups, in fact, tended to answer the first open-ended question about which groups supported their candidacy in terms of interest groups. But there are other members in the coalition, including party activists, campaign volunteer workers, newspapers, and campaign contributors. A list of the politician's coalition members would be incomplete without reference to these groups, even though they may overlap both with the interest groups and with each other to an extent. The original question, therefore, was extended by probing, primarily to discover the extent of the candidate's newspaper support and the major sources of his campaign finances.[4]

Newspapers. Politicians were asked simply whether or not they had any newspaper endorsements and if so, by which newspapers. The answers vary partly according to whether the candidate won or lost. Winners tend more than losers to indicate better newspaper support for their campaigns. Some 40 percent of the losing candidates said they had no newspaper endorsements, compared with only 16 percent of the winners. Although there may be some degree of rationalization here, with losers to an extent blaming their defeat on the press, respondents in this case may be reporting the situation as it exists in fact. Decisive winners, who are particularly prone to report that they had good newspaper support, in general come from one-party areas where the newspapers as well as most of the elite groups are on their side, whereas decisive losers would be in the opposite position.

This difference between winners and losers, however, is evident only among Democrats. Only one Democratic winner said he had no newspaper endorsements, but eight of the sixteen Democratic losers indicated that they were without newspaper support. Similarly, only one Democratic loser said that he had "good" newspaper support (more than a scattering of newspapers in the district), whereas ten of the sixteen Democratic winners felt that they had good support. In marked contrast, Republican winners and losers are

about the same: nine of the sixteen Republican winners
indicated that they had "good" newspaper support and
seven of fourteen Republican losers so indicated. Win or
lose, Republicans tend to feel that they have relatively
good newspaper support, but Democratic losers feel
rather strongly that the newspapers were not only non-
supportive but actively against them. Again, although
there are no data reported in this study to directly test
the proposition, these beliefs about newspaper support
could be accurate reflections of reality. It does seem
likely, in fact, that Democratic losers—especially in
districts heavily against them—would not be given
newspaper endorsements, whereas Republican losers
might not be in such a position as often.

Editorial endorsement is not the only or even the
most significant type of support a newspaper can give
to a candidate for office, as several politicians pointed
out. One said:

> I had most of them. But the editorial backing does not
> help unless they give you a story every day and push it.
> Five percent of the readers read the editorial page. And
> when it comes out two or three days before the election,
> it doesn't help much.

Many unsuccessful candidates, particularly Democrats,
were quick to point out the same thing. Not only were
they denied support in the editorial columns, but they
also felt they had been unable to obtain coverage of
their campaigns in the news columns. One Democratic
loser complained that voters would be well informed
"if the papers would print our releases, but the newspaper editors are Republicans and just won't print the
release." Whether or not the complaint was well founded
in fact, it was fairly common for unsuccessful candidates
who felt they did not have good newspaper support to
mention what they regarded as unfair treatment at the
hands of the press.

The type of office sought, whether the state legislature or a higher-level office such as congress or a statewide office, also enters into the candidates' assessments of their degree of newspaper support. Generally speaking, with both party and election outcome (win or loss) controlled, politicians at the higher level report better newspaper support than do those at the state legislative level. The differences between higher-level candidates and state legislative candidates, however, are accentuated for Democrats and for losers. Only one Democrat who ran for higher-level office, for instance, stated that he had no newspaper endorsements, whereas half of the Democrats running for the state legislature indicated that no newspaper supported them. Similarly, 64 percent of the losers at the legislative level indicated that they had no newspaper support and only 19 percent of the losers at the higher level were without endorsements.

Our data (see Chapter 2) indicate that candidates for the state legislature felt voters were much less interested in their races, less informed about the campaign, less aware of the issues and the candidates, than did candidates for the higher-level offices. Much of this analysis of the differences between the types of office was based on the notion that the campaigns for higher-level offices are more in the public eye and especially are reported more extensively in the press. The findings reported in the preceding paragraph demonstrate that as a matter of fact politicians do tend to view their press support in this way. We are gradually amassing evidence that suggests that candidates for the state legislature, unlike candidates for higher-level offices, operate in something of a felt vacuum, a situation in which they are comparatively neglected by the press and by the voters.

Finance. Financial contributors may also be considered coalition members. But this study does not explore the matter of campaign finance extensively, for two reasons. First, the financing of a campaign is an important topic in itself, deserving much more extended treatment than this study could allow. Second, the question of sources of financial support is a very delicate matter. One interview with a politician is not a satisfactory way to obtain either detailed or accurate information about campaign finance. The sources of candidates' finances, therefore, were considered only peripherally.[5]

There are rather sizable differences between the two parties in terms of the major source of financial support. All the candidates who said that their major source of financial support was an interest group or groups were Democrats, indicating the importance of organized labor to many Democratic candidates. (This group of respondents constitutes about one-fifth of the Democrats interviewed.) In contrast, 43 percent of the Republicans and only 13 percent of the Democrats indicated that their political party was their major source of funds. This situation can probably be accounted for by the Republican financing apparatus, to which several Republicans and even a few Democrats referred. The Republicans in Wisconsin have apparently achieved a degree of centralization in financing such that contributions are given directly to the party and then passed along to the candidates the party feels are most in need of the money and in whose races the party has the greatest chance of victory. The Democrats apparently have no such apparatus, at least none as developed as the Republicans'. The party differences in financing persist even when election outcome (win or loss) and type of office (higher-level or state legislative) are controlled. Interestingly enough, the same pattern of party difference in campaign finance has been discovered in at least one other state. Hugh Douglas Price writes that

Massachusetts Republican finances are highly integrated through the state committee, but that the Democratic state committee does not play such a central role.[6]

As in the case of newspaper support, there are differences here between the state legislative and the higher-level candidates. Those running for the state legislature have more difficulty than those running for higher-level office in finding outside sources of money and often must finance their campaigns primarily from their own pockets. Nearly one-third of the state legislative candidates said that their own personal resources were the major source of finances for their campaigns, whereas only 13 percent of the higher-level candidates did. This difference may be due not only to the possibility that discovering outside sources of funds is more difficult for the state legislative candidates, but also to the fact that a campaign for the state legislature costs less and hence can be more easily financed from personal resources.

EXPECTATIONS AND REASONS
FOR SUPPORT

It is common in popular discussion about electoral politics to speak of a candidate's promise of something in return for a given group's support. In one formal theory of political coalitions,[7] these promises, called side-payments, are used by a coalition builder to attract people to his side. Among the kinds of side-payments available for distribution to potential supporters are the threat of reprisal, payments in money, promises regarding present or future governmental policy, and emotional satisfaction for the coalition members.

This study investigates two questions related to side-payments: the types of rewards coalition members receive as reported by the candidates for office and the extent to which the politicians view the process as one of offering favors in return for support. In order to investigate these questions, after a simple listing of the respondent's coalition members was obtained, he was asked two questions about each of the coalition members he had mentioned: (1) "Can you tell me *why* they support you?" and (2) "Do you feel that they expect something of you in return for their support?" Thus, for example, if the respondent said that labor, volunteers, and some newspapers supported him, he was asked the two questions first about labor, then about the volunteers, then about the newspapers. In this way, separate judgments were obtained for each coalition member mentioned.

It is important to note that respondents were assessing only their own supporters. Politicians view their own supporters and the supporters on the other side very differently.[8] It would make a considerable difference, for example, if a business-oriented legislator or a labor-oriented legislator were telling whether or not labor expects anything of a candidate in return for its support. In this study, the politician's own coalition was the main point of interest, and he therefore was asked questions about his own supporters. This does not mean that more "objective" assessments of political groups were obtained. In fact, the judgments reported here may not conform closely to reality. But the candidate's own cognitions, realistic or not, are among the important influences on his behavior.

Reasons for Support. It would have been difficult to obtain an assessment of the content of the side-payment that coalition members receive if respondents had simply been asked a question like "What do you offer them in return?" or "What do they receive in return for their support?" The answers quite likely would have been "I offer them nothing" or "I make promises to nobody." In fact, this kind of answer was often given to the question about what coalition members expected of the politician, as reported later. The subject was therefore approached by asking why the candidate thought the coalition member supported him. The assumption was that the perceived reason for supporting a candidate would be closely connected with whatever side-payment the politician believes the member receives. If, for example, a person joins a coalition because the politician's stands on matters of policy are much like his own, then it could be said that the person receives a policy reward in the form of having a legislator in office who votes in a manner of which he approves, provided his candidate is elected.

Reasons for supporting the candidate were classified into the following two categories: (1) policy reasons, including votes in the legislature, agreement on matters of public policy, agreement on political "philosophy" or "viewpoint"; or (2) personal reasons, including personal friendship, the politician's experience or background, the supporter's own personal satisfaction, the feeling on the part of the supporters that the candidate is "one of them"—a member of their group. The rationale for this classification is basically a concern about policy outputs in the political system. If coalition members are thought to be motivated by policy considerations, this fact may have some impact on the politician's decisions about what policy stands to take, including stands in the campaign and decisions about how to cast a vote. If, on the other hand, coalition members are thought to be interested in more personal rewards such as emotional satisfaction, this sort of side-payment probably has less effect on the politician's stands on matters of public policy.

A summary of the politicians' responses appears in Table 3-2. In most cases, slightly more than half the respondents indicated that the group in question supported them for policy reasons, and the remainder cited personal reasons. This is true of the candidates' judg-

TABLE 3-2

Perceived Reasons for Group Support

Reason	BUSINESS	FARMERS	LABOR	NONECONOMIC	VOLUNTEERS	NEWSPAPERS
				Group		
Policy	55%	59%	81%	52%	34%	57%
Personal	46	41	19	48	66	43
	101%*	100%	100%	100%	100%	100%
n	22	17	32	27	50	35

* Rounding error.

ments about business, farmers, noneconomic groups, and newspapers. Responses about the other two groups, labor and campaign volunteers, however, do not fit into this generalization. Candidates who have labor support believe that labor is highly policy-oriented. Many of them mentioned a personal interview held with the candidate, in which positions on issues of public policy were discussed. When asked why labor supported them, 81 percent of these respondents cited policy reasons. In contrast, only 34 percent of the politicians stated that their campaign volunteers supported them for policy reasons. The remainder emphasized personal friendship, personal satisfaction from political participation, and the like.

If a politician thinks that a coalition member supports him for personal reasons only, we might speculate that he has less reason for taking that member's policy attitudes into account when deciding on issues of public policy either as a campaigner or as a governmental decision-maker than if he thinks that the member is motivated to support him by policy considerations. This attitude would be especially expected according to the rule of anticipated reactions mentioned at the end of Chapter 2. As he formulates his policy positions, a politician is more likely to anticipate the reactions of those groups in his coalition that he believes support him for policy reasons than of those he perceives as not overly interested in public policy. It appears, therefore, that business, farmers, noneconomic groups, and newspapers could be expected to have this sort of indirect influence over the policy positions of slightly more than half the candidates they support. In the case of organized labor, this potential for indirect influence is much higher, but campaign volunteers as a rule apparently provide comparatively little policy guidance for candidates.

This speculation on the possible importance of these perceived reasons for support does not necessarily imply that politicians with labor-oriented coalitions are "controlled" by labor in some sense. A conclusion like this would depend upon the fulfillment of such other conditions as the politician's believing that labor is indispensable to his victory, that labor demands 100 percent obedience to its wishes, and that labor's demands were in conflict with his own policy views. These conditions are not met for most of the respondents with labor-oriented coalitions. But the data presented here do point to the potential for influence that labor groups have and the lack of potential that campaign volunteers have compared with the rest of the supporting groups.

The degree to which a constituency influences the behavior of a governmental policy-maker may be somewhat greater than has often been assumed, because winners have a relatively high estimate of the degree of voter involvement (see Chapter 2). In considering the matter of coalition support, we noticed many further sources of issue cues from the district. Even if one were to concede that a politician receives virtually no issue cues from rank-and-file voters, he could still receive many cues from his constituency. A politician's constituency, after all, is composed not only of rank-and-file voters but also of various elite groups, including his coalition members. Many of the policy cues he receives from these people may be of great importance to him because they come from his active supporters.

The fact that beliefs about labor and business differ so widely might lead one to suspect that there are considerable differences between the beliefs of candidates of the political parties about other coalition members as well. This suspicion is confirmed in fact. Table 3-3 gives

TABLE 3-3

Party Differences in Perceived Reasons for Support of Noneconomic Groups and Newspapers

Reason	*Noneconomic*		*Newspapers*	
	DEMOCRAT	REPUBLICAN	DEMOCRAT	REPUBLICAN
Policy	77%	29%	75%	33%
Personal	23	71	25	67
	100%	100%	100%	100%
n	13	14	20	15

the differences between candidates of the two parties on the reasons for which they believe noneconomic groups (like lodges, clubs, ethnic groups, and educators) support them, and the reasons for which they think newspapers support them. The total number of responses is small, but the differences are striking. Democrats believe that the group in question supports them for policy reasons, and Republicans tend to believe that the group supports them for personal reasons. This finding is true for every coalition member except campaign volunteers, where no party differences emerge.

Differences with regard to reasons for the support of campaign volunteers do emerge, however, between the candidates for the state legislature and those running for higher-level office. In general, volunteers are thought to be only slightly policy-oriented. Yet fully half of the higher-level candidates see their campaign volunteers as supporting them for policy reasons, but only three state legislative candidates (14 percent) do. This difference between levels is the same for both Democrats and Republicans. There are differences in the same direction in the cases of business and farmers, but the numbers are too small to warrant any statistical statement of the relationships.

The notion that higher-level candidates live in a more policy-charged world than legislative candidates (at least by their own account of it) is further bolstered by the degree of ideological reference in their remarks about their supporters. Respondents' answers about the reasons for group support were simply scanned for any reference to ideology, such as left and right, liberal and conservative, "their viewpoint," "their thinking." Higher-level candidates are much more likely to mention such an ideological dimension in their judgments about the reasons for groups' support. Only 23 percent of the candidates for the state legislature used any ideological terminology, whereas 53 percent of the candidates for the higher-level offices did. It is interesting, however, to note how little reference there was to ideology even at the higher level.

There is evidence that the relatively rural area of the state differs from the relatively urban area. In every instance—business, farmers, labor, noneconomic groups, campaign volunteers, and newspapers—respondents from the more urban southeast portion of the state are much more likely to cite policy reasons for the group's support than those from the more rural and small-town northwest. In the case of business, for example, only one respondent from the southeast section said business groups supported him for personal reasons, whereas eight of the eleven respondents from the northwest section so indicated. Similarly, in the case of labor, only one southeastern respondent cited personal reasons for support, whereas four of the twelve northwestern respondents did, despite the heavy emphasis on labor's policy motivation overall. Responses for the rest of the coalition groups were similar. The politics of the rural and small-town areas are apparently viewed as much more personalized, whereas the politics of the urban areas are more policy-oriented, at least at the elite level.

One final question might be raised with regard to these politicians' beliefs about coalition support: To what extent are the beliefs about coalitions related to the beliefs about voters? It is conceivable that some politicians are generally prone to view the world in policy terms, so that they would have both a high estimate of voter interest, information, and issue awareness and a belief that coalition members support them for policy reasons. Other politicians might be expected to view the world in nonpolicy terms, and to have a low estimate of voter issue awareness and a belief that coalition members have nonpolicy motivations.

No consistent relationship between voter and coalition beliefs emerges, however. If anything, the candidates who rank issues as first in importance with voters tend to believe that their supporters are motivated by nonpolicy considerations more than those who rank party or candidates as first in importance, which may be evidence of a general naïveté on their part rather than a general policy or nonpolicy mental set.

Expectations. Another feature of the conception of coalition building as a *quid pro quo* arrangement is that a politician's supporters not only have some reason for joining the coalition but they also join after some rather explicit bargain with the politician. The following sort of statement has come to be a commonplace in writings on campaigning: "Candidate X promised Y in order to get the support of voting bloc Z." According to William H. Riker's coalition theory,[9] potential coalition members not only receive side-payments, but coalition-makers offer and distribute them. We shall therefore also consider the extent to which this explicit manipulation of side-payments is characteristic of candidates for office.

Again, one must exercise some care in formulating the question designed to tap this dimension. If one simply asks, "Do you promise something in return for support?", respondents will overwhelmingly answer, "No." In order to explore this question, therefore, for each group mentioned, respondents were asked: "Do you feel that they expect something of you in return for their support?" The assumption was that a minimum condition of offering rewards in return for support would be that the politician feels coalition members expect something of him in return for their support.

Responses to the question about expectations fell into three categories. Some candidates said without equivocation that the group did expect something in return. As one put it, "Anyone does—you don't say hello to a man unless he'll say hello to you." Another candidate said, "Every person or group that supports you expects at least general consistency with their points of view." A second group of respondents stated without qualification that the coalition member in question did not expect anything in return. One politician said, "They haven't come in here asking to be paid for their support," while another said, "No. There's nothing I have to do."

The remaining respondents fell into a third, middle category. These were individuals who said that the

coalition member being considered did not expect anything other than fairness, good representation, an audience for their problems, a vote in accordance with the
politician's own convictions, minor favors, or other
things that the politician felt were of relatively little
consequence or could be granted without great trouble
or compromising of his principles. The following are
examples of responses in this "No, but . . ." category:

> No, other than fairness.
>
> No, except proper representation.
>
> No, other than the right to be heard on a particular
> question.
>
> Nothing other than honest representation.
>
> Nothing real big. Things I'd do for anybody.

One Democrat put it very well: "They just expect me
to be a good liberal, and that's no burden at all. That's
why I came here." The respondents in this "No, but
. . ." category believe that coalition members do expect something of them, but only things these politicians
would do anyway. In other words, they need not be
promised anything in return for their support. All the
candidate feels he need do is be himself, that that will
suffice.

The distributions among these three categories for
each coalition member mentioned by the respondents[10]
appears in Table 3-4. Campaign volunteers are again
believed to be very different from the other coalition
members. Not only are they considered less motivated
by policy concerns than other members, but they are
also thought to expect less from the candidate. Although
labor was thought to be much more policy-oriented
than other coalition members, politicians with labor in
their coalitions do not feel that labor expects more than
other groups expect. Generally, a third or more of the
respondents believe that the coalition member expects
nothing in return for his support. A quarter to a third

TABLE 3-4

Perceived Expectations of Coalition Members in Return for Support

			Group		
Expectation	BUSI-NESS	FARM-ERS	LABOR	NONECO-NOMIC	VOLUN-TEERS
Yes, expect something	30%	35%	26%	16%	5%
No, but . . .	40	29	42	40	30
Nothing	30	35	32	44	66
	100%	99%*	100%	100%	101%*
n	20	17	31	25	44

* Rounding error.

of the respondents at most believe without qualification that their coalition members expect something in return. Consistently, 30 to 40 percent of the respondents feel that the coalition members expect only things that politicians grant as a matter of course without cost to themselves.

Perhaps more candidates do not feel that their supporters expect something of them because "expectation" is identified with "pressure" in the minds of politicians. As Bauer, Pool, and Dexter point out, a congressman feels pressured only when he believes that he is being threatened. Generally, the word "pressure" is reserved for activities of opposition interest groups.[11] The interests of one's own coalition members, therefore, would not be considered pressure, and to the extent that expectation is identified with pressure, politicians would not consider that their coalition members expected anything of them or at least anything "out of the way" or "other than normal." Several respondents, in fact, pointed this attitude out, as three fascinating responses to the question about expectations of coalition members illustrate:

> I've never felt that way because I believe in organized labor and what they're fighting for. They never had to ask.

> [Asked about labor] Nope! And it's not true of the other side either. Conservative congressmen probably get very few visits from business groups. They expect you'll continue your basic political philosophy, but they just assume this. They don't come around and ask you.

> Everything that has been requested of me is from the other side of the fence.

It appears, then, that "expecting" something in return for support is believed to be done only on the other side. A business-oriented politician may feel that labor expects much from the labor-oriented politician, but the candidate with labor in his coalition will not think so. It is probably not true, incidentally, that a labor-oriented politician rarely hears from labor. Bauer, Pool, and Dexter point out that interest groups of all kinds concentrate mostly on their friends in Congress and rarely attempt to influence their foes.[12] But it is also likely that a congressman does not regard their communications as pressure or expectation of reward for support, largely because he agrees with what they have to say or regards their requests as legitimate expressions of self-interest.

In any event, relatively few politicians feel that their coalition members expect much of them in return for their support. They do not, therefore, think of the process of coalition building as one in which they offer favors to members in return for support in a *quid pro quo* arrangement. Coalition members may very well receive rewards in the form of fulfillment of their policy or personal purposes for which they support the candidate. But the candidate will not tend to feel that he has paid any large cost in order to gain their support, because the things he feels they expect in return are regarded largely as simple continuations of his normal behavior. In the mind of the candidate, then, coalition building is a process in which he adopts a stance or a pattern of behavior and groups fall in with him or not as they see fit.

It might be reasonable to expect that more candidates at the state legislative level than at the higher level would indicate that their supporting groups expect something of them in return for support. State legislative districts are smaller than congressional or statewide districts, and a larger, more diverse district may be less conducive to a feeling that any one coalition member expects a favor in return for support. Also, state legislative districts are more likely to be homogeneous, dominated by one group or a small number of groups. Legislative candidates may therefore be especially conscious of the dominant group, and the group itself may make its expectations plain.

In the cases of business, farmers, and campaign volunteers, as a matter of fact, no differences between legislative and higher-level candidates emerge. All the respondents who said that noneconomic groups expect something of them, however, were candidates for the state legislature and all but one of the candidates who stated without qualification that labor expects something in return were running for the state legislature. This last mentioned group constitutes over half the state legislative candidates who have labor support. The tendency for state legislative politicians more than those running for higher-level offices to think that labor expects something of them remains even when the variables of election outcome (win or loss) and political party are controlled. It is apparently true that at the state legislative level, organized labor does have a greater grip on the candidates they support than at the higher level, where the greater size and diversity of the district makes labor's position more tenuous. Other data reported later in this chapter suggest the same conclusion.

Variation in response to the question of expectations of farmers is explained in part by the area of the state from which the respondent comes. Candidates with farmer support from the northwest, relatively rural portion of the state are more likely than those from the southeast section to say that farmers expect something in return for their support. Three of the four southeastern candidates with farmer support stated without qualification that farmers expect nothing in return, whereas only three out of the ten northwestern candidates with farmer support do. Running in a more completely rural area, therefore, apparently results in a greater feeling that farmers expect something in return for support. In contrast to the case of farmers, candidates in the relatively urban southeast were more likely to state that other groups expected something of them in return for support than those in the northwest, except for business, for which there were no regional differences. Half the southeastern candidates said their campaign volunteers expected nothing of them in return for support, for instance, whereas 80 percent of the northwestern candidates said so.

One might expect, in view of the consistent and substantial differences between Democrats and Republicans in the reasons they give for the group joining their coalitions, that there would be party differences on expectations as well. When asked if coalition members expected anything in return for support, however, Republicans and Democrats showed neither consistent nor sizable differences, in spite of the Democrats' greater propensity to cite policy reasons for group support. It is apparently true, therefore, that the Democrats do not feel limited or pressured by their belief that coalition members support them for policy reasons. A Democrat may realize, for instance, that labor supports him for policy reasons, but this is no burden on him, since he believes in the positions taken by labor anyway. Whether or not the Democrat's belief that labor supports him for policy reasons limits the alternatives open to him in fact is a separate question. It could be that a Democrat thinks that his supporters are watching his policy positions more than a Republican does and that this belief will influence his decisions. But the politician apparently feels no discomfort over this possibility and does not believe that labor "expects" anything of him in return for their support.

One conclusion that springs from this analysis is that there is not much relationship between reasons given for a group's support and the perceived expectations of that group. As a matter of fact, when one does attempt to directly relate perceived reasons for support to perceived group expectations, results are inconclusive. I compared the reasons given by the politicians for business support to the expectations they thought business had in return for support, on the chance that those politicians who thought business supported them for policy reasons would also be the ones who felt that business expected something of them in return. I did this for other groups as well. These cross-tabulations, however, show mixed, inconclusive, and generally weak relationships at best. As one might suspect from ex-amining data already discussed, there appears to be no relationship of any strength or consistency between perceived reasons for support and perceived expectations.

RELATIVE IMPORTANCE

A politician's behavior toward a supporting group probably depends not only on his assessment of their motivations and expectations, but also on how important he thinks that group is in terms of his election chances. If he believes the group is indispensable, he probably will pay greater attention to its desires, both expressed to him and anticipated by him, than if he believes the group is of minimal importance. Respondents in this study were therefore asked the following question: "Taking this list of supporting groups again (interviewer recited the list), who would you say is most important in terms of your election chances?"

Nearly one-third (31 percent) of the respondents replied that it was impossible to say that one of the coalition members was more important than the others. The following two unusually introspective respondents fell into this category:

> I suppose in a normal election, I need all of them. I have to put together an amalgamation, even though I'm not too conscious about it most of the time. If one component were missing, I'd be in real trouble.

> I wouldn't place any order of importance. It's dangerous. You would concentrate too much on certain groups. I suppose there probably are some that have more influence, because of their numbers or something, but I never make that evaluation. You try to hold the whole thing together.

The rest of the respondents split fairly evenly in citing volunteers, party, and interest groups as being most important. Twenty-seven percent of the sample say their own campaign volunteer workers are most important to them. One said, "My campaign committee, without question. They do the work or get it done. This isn't like some other businesses. Success is a direct function of work." Another 18 percent believe that their political party is the most important coalition element. Many of those who cited party pointed to the fact that the party provides much of the campaign finances and other help. The remaining 25 percent say that the interest groups in their coalitions are most important to them in terms of election chances. These groups include business, labor, farmers, the specified noneconomic groups, and for these purposes, newspapers. (Only one respondent stated that newspapers were his most important coalition member.)

Democrats are much more prone than Republicans to cite their supporting interest groups as being the most important members of their coalition. In fact, 39 percent of the Democrats said that interest groups were most important, compared with 9 percent of the Republicans. Most of these Democrats were speaking of organized labor. This party difference is true of both winners and losers, of candidates for both the state legislature and the higher-level offices. Among Democrats, however, state legislative candidates are more likely than Democrats running for higher-level office to say that labor is most important to them. Those who indicate that interest groups are most important to them, incidentally, are not concentrated in Milwaukee County or even in the urban portion of the state, but are spread throughout the state.

As we have seen, there are considerable differences between politicians at the state legislative level and those who compete for Congress and the statewide elective offices. Table 3-5 defines these differences. Higher-level candidates, with larger and more heterogeneous districts, are likely to have a similarly large and diverse coalition. They are much less likely than state legislative candidates to make the judgment that any one coalition member is *the* most important to them in terms of their election chances. If they do make a judgment, they tend to cite their campaign volunteers slightly more than do legislative candidates. Those running for the state legislature, on the other hand, tend more than higher-level politicians to cite interest groups as most important.

TABLE 3-5

**Candidates' Judgments of Coalition Member
Most Important for Election Chances**

	Office Level	
Most Important Group	HIGHER-LEVEL	LEGISLATIVE
Campaign volunteers	33%	20%
Political party	13	24
Interest groups	13	36
All of equal importance	42	20
	101% *	100%
n	24	25

* Rounding error.

This finding is the complement of the findings (see Chapter 2) which indicate that legislative candidates feel more isolated from voters than do higher-level politicians. I have speculated that this situation may be associated with greater interest-group activity in state legislatures. There is now more evidence to explain why interest groups may have a greater place in state legislatures than in Congress: more state legislators feel that interest groups are important to them than congressmen do.

The tendency for state legislative candidates to cite interest groups as most important to their election chances is true for both Republicans and Democrats: both the Republicans who said interest groups were most important were at the state legislative level, and seven of the ten Democrats were. When one controls for election outcome (win or loss), however, the differences in Table 3-5 between legislative and higher-level politicians are evident only among the winning candidates (present incumbents). There are no sizable differences between losing candidates at the two office levels.

This leads to a consideration of the effects of win or loss on these assessments of coalition member importance. It seems apparent, first, that more winners feel that interest groups are important in swaying election outcomes than losers. Of the twelve respondents who stated interest groups were the most important coalition member, seven are state legislative winners, and the other five are scattered evenly among legislative losers and higher-level winners and losers. Thus, interest groups are not only more important at the state legislative level, but also more important where it counts: among incumbent officeholders. This finding adds some weight to the speculation presented earlier in this chapter that organized labor in particular may be in a position to exercise greater influence in state legislatures than in Congress.

Greater emphasis by winners on interest groups is precisely the opposite of the importance they place on political parties. Only one winning candidate in this study stated that the political party organization was the most important member of his coalition, whereas one-third of the losers did. This tendency for winners to downgrade the importance of the party and the losers to upgrade it, at least comparatively speaking, is true for both political parties and at both office levels. It is especially strong among Republican losers, among whom five of the eleven state that the party was most important to them. Actually, for some of the losing candidates, the political party organization may have been virtually the only friend they had in a hostile environment. In any event, whatever party loyalty one finds among incumbent officeholders and whatever party regularity one discovers in legislative roll calls, it is clearly not enforced by a belief on the part of the incumbents that the party is crucial to them in terms of their election chances.

The proportion of winners indicating that all the coalition members were of equal importance is approximately the same as the proportion of losers. It could be, however, that candidates running in close races—whether they won or lost—might be less prone than those in decisive races to choose one coalition member as most important, on the grounds that the election was so close that everyone counted and the loss of any one group from the coalition might have meant a serious loss for the candidate. In fact, there is a tendency in this direction, though it is not overly striking. Of the marginal candidates, 40 percent state that they cannot choose one coalition member as being most important, whereas 24 percent of the decisive candidates do. The difference between marginal and decisive races might be larger, actually, if it were not for the fact that four marginal candidates' answers were in a "don't know" category as opposed to only one decisive candidate's answer. In any event, however, there is some evidence that candidates in close races attempt to hold the whole coalition together without making any judgment about whether one or another member is most important. All are important.

There are some interesting relationships between this assessment of coalition member importance and politicians' beliefs about voters. First, candidates with a low estimate of voter interest and information tend to state when asked which is their most important coalition member that they cannot make a judgment, that all of them are important. For example, 58 percent of those who say that voters are not interested in the campaign also feel that all their coalition members are of equal importance, compared to 11 percent of those who think that voters are very interested. The same occurs in the case of voter information. Of those who believe voters are not informed, 44 percent say that all their coalition members are of equal importance, whereas only 14 percent of those who believe voters are very well informed say all their coalition members are equally important. This relationship is true of both winners and losers. Apparently, when a candidate believes that voters are not paying much attention, he feels he must be careful not to opt too strongly for one or another coalition member. Because he feels himself to be in a tenuous position with voters, he also feels he must not risk excluding any groups. Candidates who believe that voters are aware of the election, on the other hand, feel safe in opting for one coalition member as most important, particularly campaign volunteers or the political party.

There is also apparently such a thing as a "party set" on the part of the losers. Although the winners show no such relationship, there is a marked tendency for the losers who feel that party label is the most important of the three factors influencing voting behavior also to feel that either party or volunteers are their most important coalition member. Ten of the fourteen losers who ranked party label as most important with voters also believe that party or volunteers are the most important coalition member, but four of the nine losers who ranked issues or candidates as most important feel the same way about the relative importance of coalition members. In sum, beliefs about voters and beliefs about the importance of coalition members appear to be related.

During the interview, in order to probe the matter of coalition members' importance a bit further, the interviewer asked the respondent, "I imagine there are some people you must keep satisfied in order to win. Can you tell me who these people are in your case?" In spite of the deliberate slanting of the question to make an affirmative response more socially acceptable, only 29 percent of the respondents stated that there was someone they must keep satisfied in order to win. It would probably be disconcerting for a candidate to feel he was so obliged to some one group of persons that he depended on them for his political success. As one respondent put it, "That would be an uncomfortable feeling, having to be so dependent on one group. It would imply that you're their captive." Again, being "captive" also takes place only on the other side. As one Republican said of his supporters, "I don't know of any that demand the same obeisance that the labor leaders expect of _____ in Wisconsin." A labor-oriented representative, however, does not feel he is submitting to labor's demands in order to keep them satisfied, but rather that he is simply voting his convictions and that labor is falling in behind him. The same respondent who said it would be uncomfortable being the captive of any one group added, "That's if you're speaking of rather small groups. Naturally, if I would vote against legislation beneficial to the working man, I'd jeopardize my election." The same phenomenon is evident on the other side. A Democrat told me his opponent was controlled by the bankers, but his opponent said that he just tried to satisfy the general public.

Another reason why most politicians feel they need not satisfy any group is that many do not believe that the group leaders control any large bloc of votes or even that they control their own members. As one Democrat said, "The power attributed to groups is overrated a great deal. Even the labor groups don't influence their own members very greatly."

The other side of the question was also probed by asking, "Whose demands can you afford to pay less attention to?" Half the respondents answered that they paid attention to everybody, that nobody was slighted. "No," said one, "I even help out my opponents. Some of the people vigorously opposed to me call on me for service and favors, and I provide it with the same promptness and attenton that I give anybody. And some of them vote for me after that." At the other extreme are the 8 percent, mostly unsuccessful candidates, who said they paid attention to nobody. One of them stated, "As a practical matter, I didn't pay attention to anybody. Nobody paid attention to me." The remaining respondents did say that they paid little attention to either obvious opponents or to political ineffectuals. Thirty percent of the sample said that opponents were slighted somewhat. One incumbent said of them, "I'm not afraid of recrimination from them, because I already have it." The remaining 12 percent fit into the same category as the respondent who said, "The only ones I can think of are the kooks in either party."

It was reported earlier that Democrats are much more ready to acknowledge the importance of interest groups in their coalitions, particularly organized labor. But when asked if there was anyone they must keep satisfied in order to win, no party differences emerged. This is true with level of office controlled as well. In about the same proportions, both Democrats and Republicans reject the notion that there is someone in their districts they must keep satisfied in order to win. Similarly, there are no differences between the parties on the question of whether or not candidates can afford to pay less attention to someone. The same pattern that has appeared before, in short, emerges here. Democrats recognize labor's importance to their election chances, but do not feel especially limited by this fact. They apparently think that labor is important to them, but not indispensable.

Differences emerge between those candidates running in districts where the vote is close and candidates in districts where the election was won by over 55 percent of the two-party vote, which leads to a generalized picture of their constituencies which is probably consistent with their districts' objective characteristics. Decisive winners and losers, first of all, believe more than marginal candidates do that there is some group in their district which they must keep satisfied in order to win. Of the decisive winners and losers, 39 percent feel that it is necessary to keep someone satisfied, as compared to only 13 percent of the candidates in close districts. The converse is also true: 41 percent of the decisive candidates feel that they must pay attention to all elements in their district and slight nobody, as compared to 61 percent of the marginal winners and losers. Decisive districts, then, are apparently rather homogeneous and tend to be dominated by a single group of people that candidates feel they need to satisfy, more than are marginal districts. Once this group has been satisfied, they feel they can afford to pay less attention to someone else. Politicians running in marginal districts, however, faced with the prospect of a close election and reluctant to cite any one group that must be kept satisfied, feel they can afford to ignore nobody in their search for votes.

It was noted above that winners at the legislative level were distinctive because they particularly felt the expectations of their supporters. The same is true here. There is a considerable difference in this matter between the responses of candidates for the state legislature and those for higher office, but this difference exists only among the winners. Unsuccessful candidates at both levels tend to believe that they do not need to keep anybody satisfied in order to win, indicating perhaps their lack of experience with the demands which constituents and particularly supporters make upon officeholders. Over half the winning candidates for the state legislature feel that there is someone in their district that they must keep satisfied, whereas only one of the winners for higher-level office thinks so. Among incumbent officeholders, then, the difference between those in the state legislature on the one hand and those in Congress and the statewide offices on the other is very striking. Once again, the evidence suggests that state legislators are particularly bound in by their coalitions and by certain elements in their districts. Congressmen and incumbents of statewide offices, with their larger, more heterogeneous districts, apparently feel more freedom from coalition constraints. The difference, however, exists only among winners (incumbent officeholders), which suggests that the demands upon the politician begin to be felt only when he gains office.

Perhaps the most important finding about the relative importance of coalition members is that most politicians attempt to avoid making a judgment about it. A third of the respondents refuse to name the most important member of their coalition, and nearly another third maintain that their most important supporters are the campaign volunteers, to whom they feel little policy obligation anyway. The candidates apparently feel that they are not particularly tied to any one group both because this would be an uncomfortable feeling for them and probably because American politics is pluralistic enough that there is in fact no *one* group which would be sufficient to ensure political success in most districts, particularly in districts of any size and heterogeneity.

CONCLUSION

Politicians have very little day-to-day contact with rank-and-file voters. They do, however, interact with political elites from their district—party activists, interest-group leaders, letter-writers, newspaper editors —very regularly. Such people are a major source of cues from the constituency.

As far as the content of the coalitions is concerned, there are striking differences between the two parties. It is clear that candidates of the two political parties perceive their supporting coalitions very differently. Democrats have coalitions that include labor but not business and professional groups, and Republicans tend to have the reverse. It may be appropriate to speculate here rather broadly on the implications of these findings.

It would seem that it makes a considerable difference which party's candidate is elected. If a Democrat is elected to public office, organized labor is likely to have greater access to governmental decision-makers than if a Republican had been elected. If a Republican is elected, on the other hand, business and professional groups are more likely to have good access than if a Democrat had been elected. The willingness of a decision-maker to listen to a group, furthermore, is necessary if any attempts to influence him are to be successful, and a man will probably listen more readily to those who helped him into office than to those who opposed him. Distinctly different groups of people or segments of the electorate, then, will probably have their share of influence on governmental policy, depending upon which party wins elections. This does not necessarily mean that either party is in some sense the "pawn" of the groups that back that party's candidates, but simply that the politician's sympathetic ear is more likely to be available to those who actively support him.

To put this point into the framework of democratic theory, it seems a plausible conclusion that different people are being represented, depending on who wins the election. It appears that there is not simply one constituency, but at least two constituencies within each electoral district. A Democrat's constituency often includes labor but not business, and a Republican's constituency often includes business but not labor. A somewhat different constituency is probably being represented, therefore, depending on who gains elective office. Election outcomes, then, are likely to be of considerable consequence: which party gains control of the governmental machinery can be expected to make a difference in terms of governmental policy. Party differences in congressional voting (which have been repeatedly observed in roll call studies), for example, are probably related to the party differences in perceived supporting coalitions.

It has often been observed that American political parties are rather diffuse amalgams of essentially local parties. This study was done on Wisconsin politicians, and party differences may not only be greater in Wisconsin than in other states but are also probably greater in any one state than they are nationally. The political party label, in other words, probably has real "meaning"—in the sense of distinctive party policies and sources of support—within Wisconsin, within California, within Alabama. This meaning, however, may vary from locality to locality. Thus, when the local parties are combined into the national amalgam, party differences are likely to be somewhat obscured, since Wisconsin Democrats will be mixed with Alabama Democrats, New York Democrats, and the like. This fact does not imply that political party has no meaning, but rather that we should use both national and local frames of reference in assessing its meaning. The important distinction between national and local political parties, in short, should always be kept in mind in any generalization about United States party differences and the policy issue or representation "meaning" of American political parties.

Coalition building is not seen by the candidates as an explicit bargain between themselves and their supporters. Most politicians seem to prefer to believe that they are relatively free of their coalition and able to exercise their independent judgment in making public policy. They feel that their supporters expect something of them in a general sense, which sets the parameters of their decision possibilities—without, however, constricting their alternatives too narrowly. When it comes to assessing coalition members' relative importance, furthermore, a majority of the politicians say either that no one group is most important to them or that their campaign volunteers are. Either of these beliefs, again, has the consequence of not pinning them down very closely to any one element in their district, because campaign volunteers are thought to be motivated by nonpolicy considerations and to expect little of the candidate. Politicians also tend to state that they believe strongly that there is nobody in their district whom they *must* keep satisfied in order to win.

This does not mean, of course, that the constituency has no influence on the politician. He does depend upon his district for his job and his political future. He also receives many cues from his district, particularly from his supporting coalition and other political elites. To say that the coalition, particularly any one member, "dictates" a vote on a given bill, however, is to overestimate the degree to which the politician is normally bound in by his constituents. Rather, his coalition of supporters probably helps to set the boundaries within which he must make his decisions and to prescribe the general path that he must follow. These boundaries are narrower than those set by rank-and-file voters, but are not so narrow as to allow the politician no freedom of action.

These generalizations, of course, do not apply to every politician, and differences among politicians are perhaps more interesting than similarities. State legislators differ from congressmen; politicians in small-town and rural areas differ from those in urban areas. These differences are summarized in the concluding chapter of this book, in which material on voters, information, and strategies is integrated with the findings on coalitions to indicate the implications this study has for politics in different contexts.

NOTES

1. See, for example, David E. Truman, *The Congressional Party* (New York: Wiley, 1959); and Julius Turner, *Party and Constituency: Pressures on Congress* (Baltimore: Johns Hopkins University Press, 1951).

2. Lewis A. Froman, Jr., *Congressmen and Their Constituencies* (Chicago: Rand McNally, 1963), chap. 7.

3. *Ibid.*, p. 95.

4. I assumed that party activists and campaign volunteers would be coalition members and so did not probe for them in this part of the interview, where a simple listing of the coalition members was the object.

5. For an extensive treatment of the subject, see Alexander Heard, *The Costs of Democracy* (Chapel Hill: University of North Carolina Press, 1960).

6. Hugh Douglas Price, "Campaign Finance in Massachusetts in 1952," *Public Policy*, 6 (1955), 30.

7. William H. Riker, *The Theory of Political Coalitions* (New Haven: Yale University Press, 1962). See especially pp. 108–14.

8. It has been argued, for instance, that "pressure" is seen as existing only on the other side. See Raymond A. Bauer, Ithiel de Sola Pool, and Lewis Anthony Dexter, *American Business and Public Policy* (New York: Atherton, 1964), p. 435.

9. Riker, *op. cit.*

10. Newspapers are not included in this table because an answer concerning them was not ascertained from a sufficient number of respondents.

11. Bauer, Pool, and Dexter, *op. cit.*, p. 434. See also Frank Bonilla, "When Is Petition 'Pressure'?" *Public Opinion Quarterly*, 20 (1956), 39–48.

12. Bauer, Pool, and Dexter, *op. cit.*, p. 442.

Chapter 4

INFORMATION

Beliefs about the environment are influenced to a degree by the types of communications channels that bring cues to the person holding the beliefs. The accuracy of a politician's beliefs and any actions he may take on the basis of his beliefs, therefore, depend in part upon these sources of information. This chapter concentrates on the information the politician receives about his district.

There are, of course, a multitude of topics that could be considered under the rubric of sources of information. There are various types of information that might conceivably be relevant to several of the politicians' decisions—information about policy attitudes of voters and elites, about possible sources of support of various kinds (finances, campaign workers, media, and voters), about the likely outcome of the election, about the areas of the district which might be most amenable to manipulation by campaigning, and about a host of other matters. One could also ask about many sources of information on each of these subjects.

Because the length of the interview in this study had to be limited in order to cover all the questions of major interest, however, respondents were asked not about information on all kinds of problems, but rather solely about information related to their election prospects. Questions in the interview schedule on this subject dealt with the degree of the politician's uncertainty over the outcome of the election and the reasons for this uncertainty, his sources of information about how he would do, and the reliance that he placed on each source.

Although what has been studied here is a relatively narrow part of the topic of information gathering, it does have several advantages from a theoretical point of view. First, information about his election prospects may be of interest to the politician himself. He is, after all, concerned with gaining and holding office, and may like to know how close he is to that objective. His belief about his election chances probably influences his decision to enter the race in the first place, and may influence the conduct of his campaign and even his behavior in office should he win. The politician who thinks the race will be close, for example, may construct his campaign very differently from the one who believes he will win in a walk. Incumbent officeholders who feel uncertain about their next election may behave differently from those who feel more secure.

Second, this category of information occupies a central place in current writing on coalitions and communications. It is therefore well suited to gathering evidence on propositions in the literature. The size of winning coalitions, for example, may be dependent partly upon the degree of uncertainty in the mind of the coalition makers. Lack of perfect knowledge in the real world forces coalition builders into estimating whether or not they are winning instead of knowing. They may therefore provide for a larger margin to make up for their uncertainty about the outcome, in order to be "on the safe side." The greater the degree of uncertainty or imperfection of information about the game's outcome, William H. Riker indicates, the larger the coalition that must be built.[1] In the present context, the greater the politician's uncertainty about his election chances, the greater would be his efforts to enlarge his coalition by attracting more groups and more voters as well. The degree of his uncertainty and his assessment of the reliability of his sources of information, therefore, become important determinants of his coalition-building efforts.

Uncertainty of various kinds bulks large in several other theories of decision-making. According to Richard M. Cyert and James G. March, organizational decision-making takes place under conditions of uncertainty. One of the major propositions in their theory is that organizations attempt to avoid uncertainty by emphasizing short-run events and evading judgments about the long run—and by negotiating or controlling their environments.[2] Politicians may act in the same way. Alternatively, it could be that politicians would rather perpetuate uncertainty than avoid or reduce it, in order to keep themselves and their campaign staffs alert and working hard. Investigation of the degree of uncertainty and the means by which politicians cope with it, then, could help to discover the degree to which uncertainty reduction and avoidance are characteristic of political campaign organizations.

Sources of information investigated here may also have some relevance to the subject of communication bias in organizations and in political life. Lewis Dexter states that a congressman's conception of his district confirms itself, since he receives the most communication from people who agree with him. He is surrounded by communication which reinforces his opinions.[3] It could be that a politician running for elective office is also exposed largely to favorable communications, information which indicates that he is not only correct in his policy stands but that also indicates he is going to be the victor. Cyert and March suggest that although there is communication bias in an organization, it is detected by the organizational decision-makers and is "vitiated by a correction factor." [4] In the present context, the politician might realize the extent of bias and take it into account in formulating his judgments about his election chances and about his district. This chapter, then, will investigate the degree to which candidates for office believe there is bias in the information that comes to them. It will be important to differentiate among several sources of information, in order to see whether or not politicians feel that some sources are more reliable than others and correct for the bias in the sources that they believe are less reliable.

In short, the subject of the politician's uncertainty and information about his election chances provides a good opportunity to investigate propositions about uncertainty avoidance and information gathering, the perception of communication bias, and the sources of information from the constituency and the politician's estimation of their reliability.

UNCERTAINTY

About half the respondents in this study (48 percent) indicated that during the campaign they were fairly sure they knew how well they would do when the votes were in. The remaining politicians said they were uncertain about the outcome of the election.

This figure may not be an accurate estimate of the actual degree to which politicians were uncertain during the preelection campaign period. The fact that these interviews were taken several months after the election leaves respondents considerable room to adjust their report of uncertainty unconsciously in order to bring it into line with the undeniable outcome. Candidates who felt uncertain of the outcome at mid-campaign can look back on it and maintain that they knew all along what the outcome would be. One candidate who was defeated by an overwhelming margin, for example, stated that he never really thought he would win, but added, "But midway you start to think, 'By God, will there be a Houdini pulled here?' " If this man had been interviewed during the campaign period, he would probably have expressed considerably more uncertainty about the outcome than he did after the returns were in, when he would look foolish for having been so optimistic as to think the outcome was in doubt. Decisive winners might also feel some uneasiness as election day approaches. Thus, the fact that 52 percent of the politicians responded that they were uncertain about the election outcome probably underestimates the actual extent of preelection uncertainty.

One might expect that uncertainty about the election outcome would be related to the actual election outcome —that those who were in fact running tight races would perceive them as such, and that those who won or lost by large margins would also reflect this in their estimates of their uncertainty, even before but especially after the election. The relationship, however, although it is in the predicted direction, is modest at best. As Table 4-1 indicates, decisive winners and losers are more likely to say that they were uncertain about the election than the actual outcome warrants. As one politician who completely swamped his opponent said, "I'm uncertain. I need to be convinced." Another very seasoned politician with a tremendous amount of experience and a convincingly assured manner to accompany his experience remarked, "I don't know very much about elections. I've been in a lot of them." So while there is some greater degree of felt uncertainty on the part of the

TABLE 4-1

Uncertainty About Outcome Related to Actual Election Outcome

Degree of Uncertainty*	Election Outcome	
	DECISIVE† WINNERS AND LOSERS	MARGINAL† WINNERS AND LOSERS
Sure of outcome	56%	40%
Uncertain	44	60
	100%	100%
n	32	30

* As measured by the question "Are you fairly sure you know how well you'll do when the votes are in, or are you more uncertain on that score?"

† Decisive winners received 55 percent or more of the two party vote, and decisive losers, their opponents, received less than 45 percent. Marginal races were those won by less than 55 percent.

marginal winners and losers, many of those who ran in decisive races also exhibit a good deal of uncertainty, even after the election.

Such a statement of the findings masks a striking difference that exists between the marginal winners and the marginal losers, a difference that cannot be explained by their common tight races. Ten of the fifteen marginal losers indicated that they were sure of the outcome, but only two of the fifteen marginal winners so indicated. Marginal winners, now shaky incumbents, thus said almost to a man that they were uncertain about the outcome of the election. These officeholders, in contrast to most of their former opponents, must prepare for another election, so they apparently develop a high degree of uncertainty about the outcome of the last one as a lesson for the future to stimulate themselves and their supporters to great efforts. Marginal losers, on the other hand, probably had, to an extent, prepared themselves to lose before the election, and the outcome confirmed their preparation. Thus, they simply recall these forebodings, saying in effect, "Deep down inside, I knew how it would turn out." Interestingly, no such difference emerges between decisive winners and losers.

Despite the fact that their races were decided by over 55 percent, nearly half the politicians in "safe" districts still maintain uncertainty over election outcomes. Nearly all the marginal winners said they had felt uncertain about the outcome. These responses suggest the possibility that politicians do not necessarily attempt to avoid or reduce uncertainty, as decision-makers in other contexts apparently do. I would hypothesize, indeed, that many candidates perpetuate uncertainty because it is functional for them. As one respondent succinctly put it, "Successful candidates run scared." Taking this tack keeps them alert and working hard, and it has the same effect on their supporters. A very successful politician observed, "A candidate is always worried about the election. If he's not, then complacency and apathy set in. This attitude gets to his supporters, and that's bad." Being convinced that one will win, according to these candidates, can be as ruinous to a good campaign as being convinced that one will lose. Uncertainty about election outcome, then, may be a healthy thing.

SOURCES OF INFORMATION

The politician has several potential sources of information about his constituency, some of which he feels he can rely on and some of which he finds unreliable. He may not be overly conscious of this process of making his assessments and getting his information. Many respondents in this study, for instance, could say that they had a feeling about the election trend, but obtaining a picture of *how* they sensed the trend required a good deal of probing.

The first question put to the respondents on sources of information was an open-ended one, designed to elicit the respondent's spontaneous mention of various sources: "Can you tell me your sources of information about how you will do when the votes are in?" This question was followed by another asking whether or not he had used any of a list of sources constructed from informal conversations with campaigners and from the replies given by pretest respondents (on the pretest, see Appendix A). Respondents were asked directly whether they used the following sources: polls, party organization people, campaign volunteers, analysis of past election statistics, and the warmth or coolness of the reception they received as they were campaigning. Respondents were also asked how much they relied on each source mentioned.

For each source of information, then, the respondent either (1) received information from the source and relied on it without stating qualifications, (2) received information from the source and relied on it with some qualifications, (3) received information from the source but did not rely on it, or (4) did not receive information from the source. A summary of the sources of information and the reliance politicians place on them is presented in Table 4-2. This table is an account of the simple frequency distribution of the total sample on each of the sources. We will consider each of the sources in order.

Polls. The first sort of information about the election that generally comes to mind in this age of public opinion polling is some sort of poll, done either commercially or by the candidate's own organization. This general reliance on surveys of some sort both by the

TABLE 4-2

**Use and Perceived Reliability of Various Sources
of Information**

	Source				
Reliability	POLLS	PARTY PEOPLE	VOLUN- TEERS	PAST STATIS- TICS	WARMTH OF RE- CEPTION
Rely without qualifica- tion	13%	21%	19%	45%	57%
Rely with qualifica- tion	5	16	19	38	8
Do not rely on source	8	48	29	5	31
No informa- tion from source	74	15	33	12	3
	100%	100%	100%	100%	99%*
n	61	61	58	60	61

* Rounding error.

press and by academic researchers, however, does not seem to be true of most politicians. As Table 4-2 indicates, three-fourths of the sample said that they did not use polls. One respondent summed up the prevailing attitude: "Some say an election is just one poll after another, but I don't believe it." Another individual, asked if there was any particular reason why he did not use polls, appeared at a loss to answer the question, and finally simply stated, "It's just never done."

Virtually all polling that is done, furthermore, takes place at the congressional and statewide levels.

All spontaneous mentions of polls in response to the open-ended question about sources of information were made by candidates for the offices of United States senator, United States congressman, governor, and lieutenant governor. When probed about the use of polls, only *one* state legislative candidate said that he took polls of any kind, whereas half the higher-level candidates did. The relatively formal types of information gathering, then, are left to candidates for statewide or federal office, but even at that level, only half the candidates take polls.

The first and most obvious reason for this reluctance to use opinion polling is scarcity of resources. Polling is expensive, in terms both of money and of time devoted to it. Resources are at a premium in a campaign, especially a campaign for the state legislature, and they can be put to more fruitful use. The statewide candidates' use of polls, furthermore, is partially explained by the fact that the state political party organizations finance a certain amount of polling in which voters are asked about the major statewide candidates by name. Candidates for the state legislature and for Congress, however, do not have access to this kind of extraorganizational source of poll information, and would be obliged to finance their own. As many writers have pointed out, information costs something. If the information cost exceeds its marginal utility, then the resources are better spent elsewhere.[5] Many politicians apparently adopt this line of reasoning, at least implicitly.

Even if the resources were available, however, many politicians distrust the findings of nonprofessional polls, and even those of professional ones. Several respondents, for instance, mentioned faulty wording of poll questions as a serious difficulty in the interpretation of results. One cited a fellow candidate's unsuccessful attempt to use a telephone poll conducted by volunteers: "Many volunteers would bias it over the phone, saying things like, 'You're not going to vote against _____, are you?' " Even with a professional poll that has more or less neutrally stated questions, many candidates remark that it only tells how voters feel at that particular point in time, but "The trouble is that things change," as one of them put it. Events that take place between the time of the poll and election day may alter people's opinions, and the candidate who relies on any poll information, no matter how well it is gathered, may be caught short.

Reliance on polls as a source of information, furthermore, may have deleterious results on the campaign. As one politician said, "If you rely on a poll that shows you in the lead, you don't work as hard." Again, this respondent and others are apparently perpetuating uncertainty over the election outcome in order to keep their own efforts and the efforts of those around them at a high level. Many politicians thus agree with Lewis Dexter's argument that polls may weaken a campaign organization by promoting complacency and thus driving away campaign volunteers and financial contributions.[6]

Party Organization People.   Other bits of information about election chances are the comments made to the candidate by people in the party organization. As Table 4-2 shows, far greater numbers of candidates receive information from this source than from polls. The politicians, however, tend not to trust the information they receive from party people. Half the sample interviewed indicated that although they did receive reports from party people about how they were doing, they found these reports to be not reliable. Candidates for higher-level offices tend to be somewhat more suspicious of this source of information than are candidates for the state legislature.[7]

A number of reasons for this distrust of the party organization as an information source were mentioned in the interviews. First, many respondents indicated that party people overestimated the candidate's popularity and election chances. As one put it, "They let their eagerness run away with them." Not only do they tend to become too enthusiastic about the candidate to be objective, but they also tend to associate with other party people who feel the same way. This continual reinforcement compounds the bias. Second, the inaccuracy of the information received from party people may not even be due to their genuine belief that the candidate is doing well, but rather to their desire to encourage him. Said one candidate, "They want to cheer you up." Third, party people may have some tendency to assure the candidate that they themselves are doing an effective job on the candidate's behalf, which leads again to an overestimate of the candidate's chances in that area. One politician stated that party organizers in a given area tell him, "Don't worry about us. Spend your time somewhere else."

Candidates, like all of us, do not simply accept each bit of information coming to them at face value. Instead, they screen information according to its source and apply a kind of discount factor to sources they have found to be unreliable. Past election statistics, for example, are believed to be more indicative than party organization people, even though approximately equal numbers of politicians receive some information from each of the two sources. A few perceptive respondents explicitly stated their tendency to discount inaccurate sources of information, as the following quotations illustrate:

> You can't rely on them 100 percent. There is a weighting factor. I couldn't set down a formula, but you just do it. You take account of the person you're talking to —does he tend to be optimistic or pessimistic, is he a worrier, and so forth. You have to exercise your independent judgment.

It's what people tell you, and you have to read between the lines. See how they express it. If they say, 'Really, you're going to have no trouble here at all,' then you know you're OK. But if they say, 'It's going to be an uphill fight, but I think you'll win,' then you know you're in trouble in that area. It's a comparative analysis of what people tell you.

Campaign Volunteers. Candidates for office apparently receive less information from campaign volunteers than they do from party organization people. As one respondent put it, "I did not get information from them. I got work." Another said of his volunteers, "I didn't even ask them. We're not really concerned with how we are doing. We're more concerned with what we *can* do. You just get into it, and work as hard as you can." About one-third of the respondents indicated that they did not use volunteers as a source of information about their election chances. Nearly another third distrusted the information they did get from their volunteers, as they did that from the party people. One respondent said, "The fellows who worked for me said I had it in the bag." Again, some respondents indicated that they apply a discount factor to the information from certain people. Said one, "You learn which people you can count on and which ones you can't."

Past Election Statistics. As Table 4-2 indicates, the use of the past election statistics in the district is widely relied upon to give an indication of the district's probable present vote. Over 80 percent of the respondents said that they depend on past statistics to some degree, and nearly half of them rely on past statistics without qualification. One candidate stated, "We geared the campaign activities on what they showed." It appears, therefore, that one way of breaking out of the favorable communication that continually comes to the candidate from his organization, short of taking polls, is to examine the past voting pattern of the constituency.

Despite the heavy reliance on past election statistics that turns up in the probe question, only 18 percent of the candidates mentioned them spontaneously in response to the open-ended question about sources of information. It is likely, then, that most politicians operate with some casual notion of the political complexion of their district that must be based on past voting patterns but that is never thought to be a source of information about election prospects until it is placed in that frame of reference by a questioner. As one Democrat mentioned, "I've never really sat down and analyzed the picture. I didn't have to. That area has been predominantly Republican, and we took it for granted that we had an uphill fight all the way."

Furthermore, all but one of the candidates who spontaneously mentioned past election statistics as a source of information were losers, and nearly two-thirds were decisive losers. This finding seems entirely consistent with the congratulation-rationalization effect outlined in Chapter 2. Losers, rationalizing their defeat, say that the district was against them to begin with, whereas winners neglect past statistics as a source of information about the present election because they adopt beliefs about the constituency that center on their own personal attributes rather than on "unchanging" characteristics of the district. In the responses to the probe question about past election statistics, however, no differences between winners and losers emerge.

At any rate, whether they do it in a formal fashion or not, politicians find some analysis of the past election statistics in their district a valuable means to determine roughly what will happen in the present election and to help outline their campaign strategies. This heavy dependence on past behavior of the environment is not unusual. The business decision-makers in Cyert and

March's study, for instance, pay a good deal of attention to the past performance of their and comparable organizations in order to set current levels of aspiration and to make current decisions. The large proportion of candidates for office who place at least some reliance on past election statistics indicates that politicians behave similarly.

Warmth of Reception. Many candidates for office attempt to correct for the communication bias in their own organization by making some judgments about the reaction they are getting from rank-and-file voters as they campaign. In fact, 57 percent of the sample felt that they could judge accurately whether the people they encountered were warm or cool toward them and that this judgment was a reliable indicator of how their campaign was progressing. One even remarked, "It's the best weathervane you've got." Part of warmth of reception is also the simple recognition of the candidate. If people that the candidate meets recognize him in some fashion, especially if he is the challenger, then he may regard this recognition as an indicator that his campaign is getting across to the voters.

Many candidates, however, do not agree that this source is an accurate predictor of election trends. Although nearly all respondents indicate that they do receive information from this source, that they can see people's warmth or coolness, there is a sharp difference of opinion among them as far as its reliability is concerned. As indicated above, over half the candidates felt confident they could determine with a good deal of accuracy whether or not people would vote for them on the basis of the reaction they encountered. Another third of the respondents, however, maintained that there was the same communication bias they had noted in their supporters. As one candidate stated it, "People are friendly and nice, but you can't rely on it for votes."

Virtually everyone the candidate meets while campaigning is at least polite, perhaps friendly, and sometimes even highly encouraging. One respondent even quantified this tendency: An unsuccessful candidate, this individual had kept a notebook as he campaigned and had written down the name of everybody who said they would vote for him. He actually compiled a number of names greater than a majority of voters in the district, which led him to believe that he would win. To his surprise, however, he was defeated by a considerable margin.

The tendency either to rely on warmth of reception or to notice information from this source but to distrust it is related to election outcome. More than half the decisive losers—those who received less than 45 percent of the two-party vote—do not find face-to-face voter reaction reliable, perhaps because favorable communications they had received from that source were so clearly unrelated to the eventual election result. Marginal losers and both types of winners, on the other hand, rely on warmth of reception more, with a third or less of each of these groups stating that the information they receive from this source is not reliable.

Regardless of win or loss, candidates who ran close races differ from those who ran in districts in which the election result was not marginal. There is some tendency for decisive candidates (those who won or lost by 55 percent and over) not to use sources of information in general, and when they do use them, to believe they are quite reliable. Marginal candidates, on the other hand, tend to be more suspicious of past statistics, party people, and campaign volunteers, but still take notice of information from these sources.[8] The only exception to this generalization is the case of warmth of reception, in which marginal candidates rely more heavily on this source than decisive candidates do (by a 10-percent difference). For a number of sources of information, therefore, decisive candidates either rely on the source or do not use it at all because their margin of election is clear anyway. Marginal candidates, however, notice information from these sources, but tend to be suspicious of it because their race is close.

Finally, confidence placed in warmth of reception the candidate encounters as he campaigns may simply be part of a general personalistic style of politics. Table 4-3 shows the relationship between the reliance placed

TABLE 4-3

Beliefs on Importance of Party, Issues, Candidates Related to Perceived Reliability of Warmth of Reception

Factor Ranked First	*Warmth of Reception*	
	VERY OR SOMEWHAT RELIABLE	NOT RELIABLE, NOT USED
Party	32%	53%
Issues	8	21
Candidates	60	26
	100%	100%
n	37	19

on warmth or coolness of reception and the ranking that candidates make of the factors that influence voters' decisions. It is clear that those who rank the personal characteristics of the candidates as first in importance— above party label and issues of the election—also tend to place a good deal of confidence in voter reaction as an indicator of election chances. This relationship holds true when election outcome (win or loss) and type of office sought (higher-level or state legislative) are controlled. The relationship is most pronounced for winners and for candidates at the state legislative level. It does appear, therefore, that there is a general style of "personalistic politics" that encompasses both the candidates' evaluation of factors that influence voting behavior and the sources upon which he relies for information about the election outcome. Some candidates see politics as more dependent on them personally than others do, and this tendency influences a number of their cognitions.

Other Sources. This account of information about election chances, of course, does not exhaust the list. In response to the open-ended question about sources of information, others were mentioned.

First among these, many respondents mentioned several personal contacts they had. These included not only some of the sources we have already discussed, such as party people and campaign workers, but also other informants and personal friends. Thus the "grapevine" or "rumor mill" were mentioned as sources of information for how the candidates were doing. If the politician had done something wrong, said these respondents, the word would get back to him. When pressed as to who these informants were, one candidate said, "Not anyone in particular. I just talk. You can tell." Another remarked, "You just pay attention and know what you're doing."

As one might expect, this reliance on the grapevine takes place more at the state legislative level than it does at the levels of Congress or the statewide offices. Some 52 percent of the candidates for the state legislature spontaneously mention these various informal contacts in response to the open-ended question, whereas only 31 percent of the candidates for higher-level office do. It is also true that winners tend to mention these personal contacts more than losers do: 55 percent of winners cite them, but only 27 percent of losers do. Again winners, with their greater emphasis on personal attributes, think also of their own personal grapevine as a source of information, whereas losers, emphasizing the uncontrollable characteristics of their district instead, neglect this as a source and mention rather the past election statistics.

A wide variety of other sorts of indicators was mentioned. Some respondents said that their opponent's campaign indicated how they were doing. If the opposition is well financed, popular, and mounting what appears to be an effective campaign, one concludes that the chances for election are not as good as if the reverse were true. But if the opponent seems to be mounting an ineffective campaign, if he engages in "desperation" tactics like personal smearing and sharpening the attack or suddenly shifts his tactics, then the picture is interpreted as being brighter. Other candidates use the votes taken in high schools several days before the election as rough substitutes for polls, not to indicate who is winning, but to show how they are doing in comparison with other candidates on their party's ticket. Other politicians mention press reaction as an indicator. In sum, then, although the major sources of information about election chances are those covered in some detail earlier in this chapter, candidates did mention several others that were "dumped into the machine," as one respondent put it.

COMMUNICATION BIAS

Respondents who indicated that they were uncertain about the outcome of the election were also asked to give some reasons for their uncertainty. Half of these politicians said in reply that factors which were beyond their control and whose effects were unknown influenced the outcome. These factors included the effect of the national and state candidates on the ticket on local races, the unknown consequences of certain salient issues, and the vagaries of voter turnout at the polls on election day.

The other half of those who indicated they were uncertain about the election outcome cited communications problems and communication bias as the primary reason for their uncertainty. One respondent put it particularly well:

> The candidate himself is the poorest judge of reaction. You have to fight yourself out of the shell of your followers. All of your closest contacts are with people who are very loyal to you. You start to think that everybody's for you. This is the reason that so many candidates predict that they will win the election.

The candidate, in other words, is surrounded by favorable communication. His followers are for him, and most voters he meets are at least receptive and polite, as this respondent indicates: "I've never met people while I was campaigning who weren't going to vote for me, and you never meet people afterward who voted against you." So the politician often does not know when he is in trouble. "It's like halitosis," said one incumbent who had not anticipated his defeat. "Your best friend won't tell you."

The propensity of the candidates to cite communications problems as the reasons for uncertainty about the election outcome is clearly related to the level of office they are seeking. As Table 4-4 shows, candidates for the state legislature tend to cite uncontrollable factors such as national and state trends and voter turnout as the primary reasons for their uncertainty about the outcome. This tendency is probably a function of their feeling that they are at the mercy of national and state occurrences and/or heavily dependent upon the vagaries of voting behavior without being able to do much about it. Higher-level candidates, those who run for Congress or for state-

TABLE 4-4

**Primary Reason for Uncertainty
About Election Outcome***

| | *Office Level* | |
| | HIGHER-LEVEL | STATE LEGISLATIVE |
Reason		
Communication bias	71%	23%
Uncontrollable factors	29	77
	100%	100%
n	17†	13†

* The question: "What are some reasons for your uncertainty about how you'll do?"

† Only those who said they were uncertain were asked this question; hence, the small number.

wide office, cite communications bias as the major reason for their uncertainty, perhaps because they feel more personally in control of their situation and less at the mercy of trends in other sectors of the political system and perhaps because they believe the electorate is paying greater attention to them as individuals.

The tendency reported earlier for the state legislative candidates to be somewhat less skeptical of party organization people and campaign volunteers is consistent with their lesser emphasis on communication bias. Apparently candidates for the state legislature are generally less attentive to the problems of communication bias than higher-level politicians—they mention it less as a reason for uncertainty, they rely on party people and volunteers more, and they more often spontaneously mention volunteers and various personal contacts in their districts as sources of information. In contrast, it appears that higher-level candidates exhibit a greater consciousness about information gathering and the problems that arise from communication bias than the state legislative candidates. They tend to do more formal gathering of information, such as through polls, and they tend to distrust more the sources of information that are likely to give rise to communication bias. State legislative candidates, on the other hand, having a more personalized style of campaigning, a greater belief that they are at the mercy of uncontrollable trends, and a comparative lack of financial resources, tend to depend on the less professional sources of information that are easily available to them and tend not to recognize the problem of communication bias.

This difference between state legislative candidates and those who run for higher-level office suggests that there may be such a thing as a general disposition to be unconcerned about the problems of communication among some candidates. It does appear in fact that those who say they are sure about the outcome of the election are also more likely to trust their sources of information than those who are uncertain about the outcome. For instance, 35 percent of those candidates who are sure about the outcome of the election also rely on party organization people without qualification, whereas only 9 percent of the uncertain candidates do. Similarly, 73 percent of the candidates who are sure about the election outcome rely without qualification on the simple warmth or coolness of the reception they receive as they campaign, and 42 percent of the uncertain candidates do. The same effect occurs with reliance on past election statistics as predictors of the present election: 59 percent of the sure candidates rely on them without qualification, and 32 percent of the uncertain candidates do. There is some evidence, then, to suggest a regular patterning of beliefs about communications and information sources. Those who feel sure of the election outcome also trust their sources of information and appear less concerned about the problem of communication bias than those who are uncertain. In more general terms, perhaps there is a general "propensity to worry" dimension among candidates that is manifested in a number of these variables.

There is also some hint of a relationship between the candidates' beliefs about these matters of uncertainty, communication, and information sources on the one hand, and their beliefs about voters on the other. The greater the certainty about the election outcome, for instance, the higher the estimate of voter information: 23 percent of the candidates who are sure about the election outcome also believe that voters are "very" well informed about the election issues, but only 7 percent of the uncertain candidates do. This relationship persists even when election outcome (win or loss) and type of office sought (state legislative or higher-level) are controlled. The candidates' estimate of voter information also appears to be related to reliance on sources of information. For example, 21 percent of those who rely to some degree on the warmth or coolness of their reception as they campaign also believe that voters are "very" well informed; only 5 percent of those who place no reliance on warmth of reception believe so. These figures, though not definitive, can be taken as suggestions that the propensity of a candidate to worry or not to worry about the race may be associated in some respects with his tendency to trust or not to trust voters' capacity for judgment. Those with a low estimate of voter information appear to be more uncertain about the election outcome and to trust their sources of information less than those with a high estimate of voter information.

In summary, a candidate for elective office is surrounded by favorable communication from the "shell of his followers." Many candidates compensate for this communication bias by not relying on information about their election chances from suspect sources such as party organization people and campaign volunteers. This compensation occurs especially at the higher-level offices, where general awareness of communications problems is more prevalent than at the state legislative level. When candidates who expressed uncertainty were asked directly, "Do you tend to get a picture of your chances that overestimates your final vote total or underestimates it?" all but one said that it overestimated their final vote total, that they had been surrounded with favorable communication.

CONCLUSION

It may be helpful to draw together the sources of information into a kind of model of communications. First, the candidate knows something about the past behavior of his district, either from a relatively casual knowledge of past votes or from a more formal analysis of past election statistics. This knowledge gives him a rough idea of his election chances and of the areas within the district in which he is likely to run well or poorly.

Once the candidate has this basic idea of the complexion of his district, he receives information from a wide variety of sources. Some politicians running for higher-level offices with adequate financial resources at their disposal take polls of various kinds to provide themselves with information both about the likely outcome of the race in various localities and (perhaps more importantly from their point of view) about the kinds of governmental problems that seem to be on voters' minds. Most candidates, however, have neither the resources nor the inclination to take polls. These politicians, many of them at the state legislative level, appear to rely to an extent on the warmth or coolness of the reception they encounter while campaigning and on an informal kind of grapevine that passes unsystematic bits of information back to the candidate. Many politicians running for elective office seem aware of the communication bias problems involved in information from party organization people and active supporters and look upon information from these sources with some degree of skepticism.

All the sources of information mentioned, however, do not eliminate uncertainty for the politician. Indeed, many politicians may perpetuate uncertainty, consciously or not, in order to keep an alert and active campaign in operation.

NOTES

1. William H. Riker, *The Theory of Political Coalitions* (New Haven: Yale University Press, 1962), pp. 77, 88–89.

2. Richard M. Cyert and James G. March, *A Behavioral Theory of the Firm* (Englewood Cliffs, N.J.: Prentice-Hall, 1963), pp. 118–20.

3. Lewis Anthony Dexter, "The Representative and His District," *Human Organization,* 16 (1957), 2–13.

4. Cyert and March, *op. cit.,* p. 82.

5. See, for example, Charles C. Holt, Franco Modigliani, John F. Muth, and Herbert A. Simon, *Planning Production, Inventories, and Work Force* (Englewood Cliffs, N.J.: Prentice-Hall, 1960), p. 123.

6. Lewis Anthony Dexter, "The Use of Public Opinion Polls by Political Party Organizations," *Public Opinion Quarterly,* 18 (1954), 53–61.

7. Some 45 percent of the state legislative candidates find party people at least reliable with qualification, whereas only 31 percent of the higher-level candidates do.

8. For instance, 33 percent of marginal candidates rely on past statistics without qualification, whereas 53 percent of decisive candidates do; 67 percent of marginal candidates find party people unreliable, compared with 28 percent of decisive candidates; 40 percent of marginal candidates find volunteers unreliable, compared with 16 percent of decisive candidates.

Chapter 5

CAMPAIGN STRATEGIES

★

Relations between the governors and those they govern are not simply a matter of the influence of the people upon their representatives. Politicians are not passive observers of their districts or inert instruments of the will of their constituencies. Rather, politicians attempt to manipulate their constituencies. They try to persuade voters to cast their ballots for them, they seek to gain support and to discourage opposition, and they try to build up a combination of voters and groups sufficient to elect them. A major portion of a politician's effort to manipulate his constituency takes place during the campaign, which can be conceived of either as the short period of time before an election or as public-oriented activities in which an elected officeholder engages day in and day out. Campaigning for public office is one type of human behavior that is widely acknowledged to be "political" behavior. Continuous campaigning is probably one of the reasons that incumbents enjoy an advantage over their opponents. Citizen involvement in politics is never higher than during a Presidential campaign. On occasion, a timely and well-conducted campaign may have a major influence on an election outcome.

Most of the literature on campaigning falls into two categories. One is the considerable volume of writing aimed at reforming campaign practices.[1] The other recommends a set of optimal strategies that a candidate might use in order to achieve electoral success. Such recommendations range from the fairly straightforward "how to" treatises that advise a candidate on everything from the political speech to handshaking technique[2] to the more sophisticated recommendations based on survey research findings or game theory.[3] In short, literature on campaigning has often asked the question: "How should candidates behave?" (either in the ethical sense or in the sense of devising optimal strategies). Less literature has been devoted to these questions: "How do candidates behave in fact?" "What are the calculations that they actually do make?" In this chapter we shall attempt to contribute to our knowledge of how politicians go about formulating their campaign strategies.

IMPORTANCE AND COSTS
OF CAMPAIGNING

Right or wrong, most candidates believe that campaigns affect election outcomes.[4] "Probably most important is that you get out and work," said one candidate. "Nothing happens accidentally. It's all on purpose." This statement seems to reflect the thinking of most politicians. One repeatedly encounters in personal interviews with politicians a belief in the efficacy of hard campaigning, in the ability of a good campaigner to produce the result he wishes. Success stories are often heard about candidates who, apparently by pouring sufficient resources and effort into a campaign or by coming across a catchy gimmick, have overcome great odds to achieve electoral victory. Conversely, the proverbial incumbent who failed to see his popularity crumbling under him and who failed to work hard at the business of maintaining himself in office is also apparently much in the minds of politicians. The fact that a representative and his staff spend large portions of their day engaged in what is essentially campaigning activity is probably a reflection of their belief in the importance of and results produced by campaigning.

The campaign period itself is more important to the challenger than to the incumbent. One challenger defined his position in this way:

> We had to overcome the fact that nobody in God's name knew who I was. I'd never been in the papers, had never inherited a million dollars, was never a big athlete. That was the first hurdle—try to get some identification.

The campaign period, then, is often the only opportunity for a challenger to put his name before the voters, and for that reason it is crucial to him. But campaigns are also important to incumbents. Indeed, the opportunity to continue campaign activities throughout his tenure in office is one reason why the incumbent normally has an advantage in an election contest. As one incumbent put it, "I work at it all the time, so campaigns are nothing special." This continuous exposure to the public is something the challenger must overcome.

Incumbents, too, have an opportunity through the years to build up quite an advantage not only in exposure to the public but also in popular confidence in the job they are doing. If the officeholder handles his "cases" with dispatch, returns to the district often, and continually gets himself reported in the mass media, he may build up a considerable reputation as the man who has a genuine interest in the problems of his constituents and who will do his best to see that their complaints are alleviated and that their desires are represented in the councils of government. Some incumbents do so well at this that their opponents are flabbergasted at the disadvantages under which they are obliged to labor. One such hapless challenger remarked, "You're taking on almost a myth." Another said of his incumbent opponent, "He's just a legend."

Being an incumbent and having been actively engaged in the day-to-day affairs of government is also an advantage during the campaign period itself. Several challengers told me that they did not know the issues in any detail, and felt particularly handicapped when campaigning against an officeholder who had been dealing with governmental policy continuously. One incumbent stated his advantage this way:

> I'm sure they don't mean it to turn out this way, but after the League of Women Voters interviews me and my opponent on television, the election is over. This is the best thing they could do, because I always demonstrate my superior knowledge. I hope they continue it.

Another incumbent cited the nonpartisan, politically "neutral" League to make something of the same point:

> The League of Women Voters sends out a questionnaire. . . . On one of their questions they ask candidates to state their qualifications, and this sort of amuses me. I can say I've been in for six terms, and feel qualified for a seventh. This is a real advantage.

As the responses of these two politicians intimate, emphasis on knowledge and experience is not a neutral, nonpartisan factor in politics but confers decided advantages on some and disadvantages on others. For a number of reasons, therefore, many of them having to do with the kinds of campaigning activity in which officeholders engage day in and day out, the incumbent in an election generally holds an advantage.

Many incumbents state that even though they are not particularly worried about the outcome of the election, they still campaign vigorously. Three-fourths of the incumbent officeholders indicated that they had campaigned "very" vigorously; only one-tenth stated that they had not campaigned vigorously at all. One incumbent who said that he was not too worried and did in fact win by a tremendous margin still maintained that he campaigned "just as if I were fighting for life." Among the reasons for this tendency to campaign vigorously even if reasonably sure of the outcome is the uncertainty in politics discussed in Chapter 4.

There are several other reasons for vigorous campaigning that turn on politicians' goals in campaigning. Winning the election at hand is not the only goal. Many candidates, for instance, want to defeat their opponents by an overwhelming margin because this will discourage opposition in future elections. If a politician is interested in running for higher office, one condition for the satisfaction of this ambition may be his ability to demonstrate to party people and others that he is a "vote-getter"—that he wins decisively when he campaigns. There is also a good deal of personal satisfaction involved in winning by a wide rather than a narrow margin. Many politicians, finally, feel an obligation to their supporters and to other candidates on the party ticket, who are looking to them for vigorous campaigning. For all these reasons, then, the candidate may desire to "win big" even if he is relatively certain of the outcome and has what he regards as reasonably complete information.

Campaigning, of course, has its costs. The most obvious are those of time and money. Campaigning, according to many politicians, is terribly expensive and is becoming ever more so because of the increasing need for exposure in the mass media, particularly television. It is also very time-consuming. It was not at all uncommon for candidates to report that they had done nothing but campaign for the office they were seeking for periods ranging from a few weeks to a matter of months. As one respondent said, "The big thing in campaigning is *time* and *money*."

Another fairly obvious cost of campaigning is the toll it exacts in human energy. Many politicians report that campaigning is strenuous activity which is extremely taxing both mentally and physically. One respondent put it particularly well, if somewhat pessimistically:

> A lot of people, especially college-age people, want to get attached to campaigns. There's a lot of glamor and excitement. The first thing they learn is that there's a lot of just plain *hard work*. I had a college student working for me last time, and once I just had to dress him down for complaining of it. There's a lot of drudgery. You wear yourself right down to a nub, and it's going to get worse. We'll keep it up until one of our Presidential candidates will kill himself. It's going to happen.

An aide to a congressman remarked that after observing how hard his boss worked at the business of staying in office, he would never run for Congress himself.

The campaign is difficult not only for the candidate himself, but also for his family. It was not uncommon for respondents to mention the price paid by their families in terms of constant public scrutiny, time and effort spent in campaigning themselves, and separation from one another. Many said that their families would be better off if they were not in politics. In sum, candidates paint a picture of campaigning as a costly business, in a number of respects. A few of them, however, are still able to speak in a more humorous vein of the costs involved:

I did some going door-to-door, and I never got such a gutful of ill-conceived food in my life. People want to show their appreciation, and you get beer at one place, lemon pie at the next. You have to have a strong constitution.

These farmers are pretty touchy about getting the short end of the stick. You have to walk right up to them, and their hand is dirty, but you have to just grab that paw and hold the sonofagun tight. And you can't dance over the piles in the farmyard either.

QUESTIONS EXPLORED

This chapter is based on respondents' replies to questions centered on two subjects: the candidates' issue strategies and group appeals. On issue strategies, the interviewees were asked which issues they emphasized and why they chose them, and whether they dealt with these issues generally or in a detailed fashion. It has become common to argue that because voters are ill-informed on matters of public policy, issue appeals made in the election campaign are of little consequence. There are a number of reasons why campaign issues may instead be of considerable consequence. First, many group leaders, newspaper editors, and other "opinion leaders" in the district probably join the candidate's coalition for policy reasons. They could hardly do so if the candidate did not make evident his stands on issues of public policy, in the campaign and in other contexts. Second, as reported in Chapter 2, winning candidates tend to attribute a good deal of issue awareness to the voters. If an officeholder feels that voters are watching and holding him to account for his promises, then the stands he took in the campaign may be of some importance in explaining his decisions on matters of public policy.

Critical issues, furthermore, have been known to

have an impact on election outcomes, as the tax issue apparently did in the Wisconsin gubernatorial campaign of 1962.[5] If an issue does sometimes materially affect an election outcome and—more important—if the candidate has little notion of the conditions under which this will occur, then the issue positions he takes and the relationship they bear to the preferences of his constituents are of some importance to him, both as a campaigner and as a governmental decision-maker.

In the second set of questions, on group appeals, the candidate was asked if he made an appeal to any particular groups, and, if so, which they were and why he considered them important. To obtain information on the candidate's beliefs about the importance of very large groupings in the electorate, each respondent was asked whether he concentrated in areas where he felt he was strong or in areas where he felt he was weak. Campaigning has often been conceived of as a process of coalition building in which the candidate attempts to put together a set of supporting groups sufficient to elect him.[6] These interview questions were therefore designed to tap some of the candidates' calculations involved in building this coalition beyond those covered in Chapter 3.

Interview time was not available in this project for the other questions about campaign strategies that could, no doubt, be asked. I limited my questions to those matters of direct concern to these candidates—strategic considerations for which they would be particularly responsible. Other important strategy questions, such as scheduling and choice of the particular devices to be used (matchbooks, bumper stickers, and so forth), are often left to members of the candidate's staff. In any event, it is hoped that this study can at least contribute to the literature on campaigning some empirical data on the way candidates do in fact calculate.

GROUP APPEALS

Candidates are often viewed as consciously building a coalition of supporting groups sufficient to elect them. Respondents were asked, therefore, "In your campaigning, is there any group or groups of voters that you especially make an appeal to?" The data suggest that building a coalition by means of appeals to groups in the electorate is far from universal among candidates for office. Indeed, nearly one-half (44 percent) of this sample replied that they do not make group appeals. One of these politicians said, "I wouldn't say I attempted to put together a combination of ethnic groups or economic groups or anything of this kind. Generally speaking, I tried to appeal to one group as I would to another." A second respondent maintained, "I'm cognizant of blocs, but I don't make any special appeal. They know over the years what I stand for."

A clue to the reason for a nongroup approach to the electorate is found in the comparisons of the two political parties. As Table 5-1 indicates, Democrats

TABLE 5-1

Group Appeals and Political Party

Appeal	*Party*	
	DEMOCRATS	REPUBLICANS
Makes group appeals	75%	37%
Does not make group appeals	25	63
	100%	100%
n	32	30

tend to make appeals to groups within the electorate, whereas Republicans indicate that they do not, that they prefer instead to spread themselves evenly over the district. The reason for this party difference probably lies in the types of coalitions supporting the two parties (see Chapter 3). Because of his probable base of support, a Democrat can often put forth the image of the "friend of the working man," but a Republican is probably loath to be tagged as the "friend of the banker, businessman, and doctor." The Democrat, in other words, is able to make group appeals because the groups to which he appeals may be sufficient to elect him. In addition to labor, the Democrat is likely in most northern states to have the support of the identifiable religious, ethnic, and racial minority groups. The Republican, on the other hand, cannot make group appeals as readily because the groups to which he would appeal are not sufficient to elect him, and such appeals might in fact hurt his chances. Instead of making group appeals, he attempts to gloss over group differences and simply reach as many people as he can as individual voters.

Part of the difference between the political parties is probably also explainable in terms of the degree to which candidates believe that interest groups are the most important element in their supporting coalition. Democrats tend to believe more often than Republicans that an interest group is the most important of the coalition members in terms of election chances (see Chapter 3). It is also true that *all* the candidates who believe an interest group is most important to them make group appeals in their campaigning.

This finding about group strategy can be stated in terms of a more general proposition that is testable in and perhaps applicable to campaign strategies throughout the United States and in other democracies as well. The proposition would be as follows: Candidates whose political parties have the support of groups with numbers of members equal to or surpassing the candidates' aspiration levels for number of votes desired concentrate on appealing to these groups in order to reinforce their already strong support. Candidates whose political parties do not have such group support, on the other hand, construct an undifferentiated, nongroup, individually based appeal to the electorate. According to this proposition, for example, Democrats in many northern, urban states might characterize themselves as "Democrats and friends of the underdog," whereas Republicans would say that they "represent all of the people and deplore attempts to pit one group against another for political gain." Michigan Governor George Romney's campaign for reelection in 1966 was based on precisely this sort of appeal.

This basic proposition is bolstered by a few other bits of evidence drawn from this study. Among the relatively small number of Republicans who do make group appeals, for example, more of them make their appeal to labor but not to business than vice versa. They apparently feel that they must do something to offset their disadvantage by concentrating their efforts on labor rather than reinforcing their advantage as Democrats are likely to do. Eight of the eleven Republicans who make group appeals, furthermore, ran in close races, where they probably felt that they had to resort to every tactic available, including group appeals. In Milwaukee County, where the Republican party is decidedly in the minority, none of the Republican candidates said that they appealed to groups.

Though the numbers are too small to be worthy of statistical treatment, it may be of interest that those candidates who believe their coalition members expect something of them in return for support tend to a degree to avoid making group appeals. This is true for all types of coalition members. Apparently a politician feels somewhat more comfortable constructing a campaign based on group appeals if he feels that there will be no favor expected in return. If he does believe that a *quid pro quo* is expected, he tends to shy away from group appeals.

To turn now to broader groupings in the electorate than those to which we have referred thus far, in the folklore of politics one of the "rules" of good campaigning is that one should concentrate on areas where one is strong. As one of the respondents in this study said, "The first lesson in politics is that you campaign where you're going to get votes." If this is indeed the first lesson, then many candidates for office either never learned it or simply ignore it. When asked, "Do you concentrate on voters in areas where you think you will do well, or where you think you'll run poorly, or what?" only a third of the sample indicated that they concentrate on areas where they think they'll do well. Another third said they go where they expect to do poorly, and the remaining third maintain a relatively even spread over the district, some saying they go to wherever the population is concentrated, whether or not they would do well there.

As in the case of group appeals, the candidates' political party affiliations explain some of the variation in campaign strategy. Table 5-2 shows that though a majority of neither party depend on strong areas, Democrats tend more than Republicans to concentrate on areas where they will do well. Republicans either go to areas where they will do poorly or attempt to maintain a relatively even spread over the district. Again, because Democrats have an edge in terms of numbers partly due to the composition of their supporting coalitions, concentration on their strong areas may be sufficient. Such a strategy would not suffice for a Republican. It is also possible that many candidates in both parties concentrate on urban areas in their districts, areas of dense population concentration "where the people are." A Democrat would think of this type of area as "strong," whereas a Republican would be obliged to campaign there whether he thought it was strong or not.

Election chances also affect the strategy adopted by the candidates. Respondents were again divided into four groups according to election outcome: decisive winners (those who won by 55 percent of the two-party vote or more); marginal winners (those who received up to 55 percent); marginal losers (those who received at least 45 percent but less than 50 percent); and decisive losers (those who received less than 45 percent). Of both groups of winners and the marginal losers, one-third or fewer of the candidates said that they concentrated on areas where they would do poorly. But over half the decisive losers indicated that they did, and of the five Republican decisive losers, four concentrated on their weak areas.[7]

TABLE 5-2

Concentration on Strong or Weak Areas in District, by Party

Concentration	Party	
	DEMOCRATS	REPUBLICANS
Strong areas	39%	21%
Even spread	29	38
Weak areas	32	41
	100%	100%
n	28	29

The candidate's felt uncertainty about the outcome has a bearing on concentration of effort as well. Four of the six decisive winners who nevertheless felt uncertain about outcome concentrated on their strong areas, but only one of the eight decisive winners who

felt sure of the outcome did so. In the case of the decisive winner, therefore, uncertainty about the outcome of
the election would seem to produce a strategy of reinforcing strong areas, whereas lack of uncertainty would
allow him more room for experimentation.

Occasionally, a respondent said that going to his
weak areas was a mistake on his part and maintained
that he would have received more votes if he had concentrated instead on his areas of strength. One respondent cited an amusing instance of this:

> I lost one election by meeting the wrong people. _____
> County is full of Illinois people in the summer, and you
> talk your fool head off and never get votes because
> they're not residents.

But perhaps more to the point, many of these candidates
faced races in which concentrating on areas where they
were strong would not be enough in a district predominantly against them. Some of them were even faced
with a district in which there were few or no areas in
which they could think of themselves as running well.

Though the numbers are again too small for statistical treatment, it appears that candidates who believe
their coalition members support them for personal
reasons tend to campaign in their weak areas more
than do those who think that they get support for
policy reasons. Apparently, if a candidate believes that
personal considerations motivate supporters, he probably will campaign in potentially hostile areas because
he feels that policy criticism is less likely. Candidates
who believe that support is policy-motivated, however,
shy away from their weak areas, apparently on the
grounds that their issue positions could drive away
supporters. This hypothesis is admittedly tenuous, but
the relationships are consistent enough to be worth
reporting.

ISSUE CHOICE

Respondents were asked first simply to name the issues they particularly stressed: "In this last election, which issues did you emphasize?" Answers were classified according to a conservative-liberal distinction. About a quarter of the sample stated that they made an essentially conservative issue appeal, emphasizing such issues as the size of the budget and the level of government spending, efficiency in government, and taxation designed to promote business activity. Some 30 percent of the sample emphasized issues classified as liberal, such as the need for programs in education, welfare, and civil rights. Politicians rarely position themselves on both sides of the liberal-conservative dichotomy: only five respondents emphasized both liberal and conservative issue positions. Nearly a quarter of the sample (23 percent) indicated that there was no emphasis on issues of public policy in their campaigns, that they stressed instead their personal characteristics, their experience, and similar factors. The remaining 13 percent of the respondents spoke of issues that were essentially neither conservative nor liberal, such as highways, highway safety, and conservation. Many politicians in these last two categories were apparently avoiding a commitment on issues that could conceivably be detrimental to their election chances. One candidate said, "Highway safety—you can't get hurt on that."

As one might expect, the political party of the candidate is closely related to the type of issue appeal he makes in his campaign. Not only do the parties differ according to the kind of supporting coalitions, they also differ markedly in the issue positions they present to the electorate. As Table 5-3 shows, Democrats tend strongly to emphasize liberal issue positions, and Republicans tend to emphasize conservative ones. When candidates emphasize neither, Republicans tend to avoid issue emphasis altogether, concentrating on their personal attributes and the like. Democrats, on the other hand, tend to take stands on issues of public policy that are either both liberal and conservative or noncontroversial. This last finding is perhaps due to the Democrats' greater tendency to perceive their supporters as joining their coalition for policy reasons, as opposed to the Republican tendency to cite personal reasons for coalition members' support (see Chapter 3).

TABLE 5-3

Political Party and Issue Emphasis

	Party	
Issue Emphasis	DEMOCRATS	REPUBLICANS
Liberal	55%	7%
Conservative	3	47
Both, or noncontroversial	29	13
No policy emphasis	13	33
	100%	100%
n	31	30

The party differences in issue appeal probably reflect the differences in coalition support. Table 5-4 demonstrates the direct relationship between coalition support and issue appeal. Those candidates with business-oriented coalitions tend to make a more conservative appeal than the others; those with a labor-oriented coalition, a more liberal one; and those with a coalition that straddles the labor-business dichotomy also straddle the liberal-conservative points of view in their issue appeal.

The associations among party, coalition, and strategy come full circle when one examines the relationship

TABLE 5-4

Supporting Coalition and Issue Emphasis

	Supporting Coalition		
Issue Emphasis	LABOR-ORIENTED	BUSINESS-ORIENTED	ANOTHER COALITION
Liberal	59%	0%	19%
Conservative	5	54	19
Both, or non-controversial	27	8	31
No policy emphasis	9	39	31
	100%	101% *	100%
n	22	13	16

* Rounding error.

between the two types of strategies, issue choice and group appeals. As Table 5-5 indicates, those who emphasize conservative issue positions also avoid group appeals; those who take liberal issue positions also make group appeals.

Choice of issues is also related to candidates' beliefs about the motivations of coalition members. Generally, if the candidate believes his coalition members support him for policy reasons, he is more likely to opt for liberal or conservative issue positions than if he believes that they support him for personal reasons, in which case he tends to opt for issue stances that are not clearly conservative or liberal. Of the twelve candidates who said that business groups support them for policy reasons, for instance, seven emphasized conservative issue positions, whereas only two of the ten candidates who said business supported them for personal reasons emphasized conservative positions. Results were similar

TABLE 5-5

**Relationship Between Issue Choice
and Group Appeals**

| | *Issue Choice* | | |
	LIBERAL	CONSERVA-TIVE	NEITHER*
Does make group appeals	74%	33%	59%
Does not make group appeals	26	67	41
	100%	100%	100%
n	19	15	27

* "Neither" includes those who discuss both liberal and conservative positions, those who emphasize noncontroversial issues and those with no policy emphasis.

for the other supporting groups. Choice of issues is also linked to ideological dimensions in responses about coalition members. Three-fourths of the candidates who had some ideological content (left-right, "their viewpoint," etc.) in their answers about coalition support also take either liberal or conservative issue positions, whereas less than half (43 percent) of those with no ideological content in their coalition answers are unambiguously on the liberal or conservative side. Whether or not politicians think of their supporters in policy terms, then, is reflected in their choice of campaign strategies.

We have noted that Republicans with business-oriented coalitions tend to avoid group appeals, apparently because they could hardly appeal to a sizable number of voters on that basis. The same tendency is exhibited with reduced strength here. As Tables 5-3 and

5-4 show, Republicans and those with business-oriented coalitions who do not emphasize conservative issue positions in their campaigns have a strong tendency to avoid questions of public policy altogether. Both tables show, however, that about half of each group (that is, Republican candidates and candidates with business-oriented coalitions) emphasize conservative issue positions. There is also no evidence in this study to indicate that fewer Republicans take conservative issue stands when the race is close than when it is not, in marked contrast to Democrats, who demonstrate a decided tendency to avoid simple liberal appeals as the race becomes closer and to concentrate instead on safe issues like conservation and highway safety. Apparently some candidates choose campaign strategies in accordance with their own values about which governmental policies are best, as well as the effects that strategies may have on the electorate. It may be relatively easy psychologically for some candidates to refuse to appeal to groups in order to win votes, but the desertion of one's views on matters of public policy seems more difficult.

Evidence for the importance of policy values as determinants of campaign strategy is found in the respondents' answers to the question, "Why did you choose these [issues]?" One might expect that a politician would answer in terms of some consideration involving his acceptance or rejection at the polls. He might say that the issue had political appeal, that it was of great concern in his district, that his position on it was popular, or something of the sort. Yet 41 percent of the respondents did not mention such considerations in their answers; they indicated instead that they chose the issue because they felt it was an important matter of public policy. There is an element of rationalization that accounts for part of this finding: candidates who lost the election were somewhat more likely to state that they chose their issues for policy importance than were winners, saying in effect, "I did what was right no matter what the consequences." Part of this difference between winners and losers, however, may not be mere after-the-fact rationalization; it could be that some candidates who lost by a wide margin were fairly sure that they would lose early in the game and decided to at least "speak their mind." In fact, 60 percent of the decisive losers did indicate that they chose their issues on the basis of policy importance.

We speculated above that some of the candidates who took conservative issue positions may have done so for essentially policy reasons, rather than for reasons involving their desire to be elected. In response to the question about why they chose the issues they did, 60 percent of those who emphasized conservative issues indicated that they had indeed done so for reasons of policy importance, compared with 42 percent of those who emphasized liberal issue positions. If one considers only the election winners, six of the eight winners who emphasized conservative issues said they did so for policy reasons, whereas only one of the eight liberal winners indicated the same. It does appear, then, that policy values, especially of the conservatives, affect their campaign strategies.

Respondents were asked not only which issues they chose to emphasize, but whether they presented their chosen issues in a general or a detailed fashion. Lewis A. Froman maintains, "Strategy number one is to be general," because getting into specific issue discussions will lose the attention of the audience and will appeal to an overly narrow segment of the electorate.[8] In this study, slightly over half the respondents (54 percent) said that they presented their issues generally. Another quarter said that they dealt with their issues in detail, and the final quarter indicated that it depended on the audience to which they were speaking or the medium through which they were attempting to reach the public.

One might expect to find a relationship between this strategy dimension and the candidate's belief about the degree of interest and information among voters. If the politician felt that voters were politically interested and informed about the issues, he might be expected to deal with issues in a more specific way than if he felt the voters were paying no attention. But the study results are mixed. Those who believe that voters are highly interested in their campaign also present issues specifically: ten of the fourteen candidates who discuss issues in a detailed fashion also believe that voters are "very" interested in their campaign. The same relationship does not emerge between strategy and perceived degree of voter information, however.

Presentation of issues does vary to some degree according to whether or not the candidate believes that members of his supporting coalition expect something of him in return for their support. Consistently, when queried about several different kinds of coalition members, politicians who feel that their supporters expect something in return attempt to stay general in their issue appeals in order to avoid pinning themselves down to any specific promises to which their supporters can then hold them. Those who believe their supporters do not expect anything in return, on the other hand, do not feel so constrained and engage in more specific issue discussion. So it does appear that issue presentation is designed in part to provide an umbrella under which coalition members may gather, provided that the candidate believes such an umbrella is necessary.

Whether the candidate makes a general or specific issue presentation depends in part on the type of race he faces. The candidate who has a decidedly uphill fight tends to stay general, since becoming specific on issues of governmental policy is only likely to alienate people in a district that tends to be against him anyway. His

opponent in that district tends to adopt the same strategy: relatively sure he will win, he simply keeps his
name before the voters without getting involved in
complicated issue discussions (see Table 5-6).[9] Candi-

TABLE 5-6

Type of Race and Issue Presentation

Presentation	DECISIVE WINNERS AND LOSERS	MARGINAL WINNERS AND LOSERS
General	65%	43%
Depends	16	30
Detailed	19	27
	100%	100%
n	31	30

dates in more marginal districts, however, must run a
more active campaign. People in this type of district
are more likely to be interested in the campaign and
the news media are more willing to cover it. Marginal
candidates therefore feel they must vary their presentation a good deal, which necessitates discussing issues
in greater detail, in order to keep the media and the
public interested. Furthermore, when one examines the
cases of the candidates who indicate that they concentrate their campaign on areas in their district where
they will do poorly, fully 70 percent of them indicate
that they deal with their issues generally, compared to
45 percent of the candidates who either concentrate on
their strong areas or attempt an even spread over the
district. Again, it is difficult for a candidate to get
specific in areas where people are likely to be against
him, although it is easier in other sorts of areas.

Presentation of the issues also varies according to
the office for which the candidate is running. As Table
5-7 shows, candidates for the state legislature deal with

their issues in a more general fashion than do candidates for the higher-level offices—United States senator and congressman and such statewide elective offices as the governorship. State legislative candidates feel that the public and especially the press will not pay much attention to them and that in order to get any publicity at all they must "keep it short." Candidates for the higher-level offices, on the other hand, rely on the media much more than the state legislative candidates do. In order to place releases in the papers and on television and radio on a fairly regular basis, they must vary their campaign and get specific enough to "make news." [10]

TABLE 5-7

Type of Office and Issue Presentation

	Type of Office	
Presentation	STATE LEGISLATIVE	HIGHER-LEVEL
General	63%	45%
Depends	27	19
Detailed	10	36
	100%	100%
n	30	31

Direct evidence of the greater importance of the media in the calculations of the candidates for higher-level offices appears in the respondents' answers to the question asking why they presented their issues generally or specifically. As Table 5-8 indicates, state legislative candidates are prone to cite the audience toward whom the campaign is directed. They tend to say that people would not be interested, that they would lose their audience if they discussed issues in detail. Candidates for higher-level offices, on the other hand, emphasize

TABLE 5-8

Reasons for Issue Presentation

	Type of Office	
Reasons	STATE LEGISLATIVE	HIGHER-LEVEL
Audience considerations	65%	44%
Nonaudience considerations	35	56
	100%	100%
n	26	27

such nonaudience considerations as the need to tailor their appeal to the media. Their campaigns are directed more at voters *through* the mass media than at voters directly, at least compared with the campaigns run by legislative candidates.

CONCLUSIONS

We have discovered that a number of variables are rather closely associated—the candidate's political party affiliation, the type of supporting coalition he has, and the campaign strategies of issue choice and group appeals. The causal paths among the variables are not entirely clear. It could be, for instance, that an individual (later a candidate) who believes in certain policy positions decides to participate actively in the affairs of the party of his choice, the party that already has the support of like-minded groups. The candidate could also be deliberately structuring his issues and group appeals to reach certain types of people. Although the possible causal interpretations are not tested here, the fact that the variables are closely associated is clear.

This association makes it possible to isolate two

clusters of candidate attributes and strategies, each connected with one of the political parties. The Republican
candidates tend to have supporting coalitions that include business and professional groups but do not include labor. Given this supporting coalition, Republicans tend to construct a nongroup, undifferentiated appeal to the electorate and to emphasize conservative
issue positions. Democrats, on the other hand, with
labor-oriented supporting coalitions, tend to emphasize
liberal issue positions and to make appeals directly to
groups. We may hypothesize that this tendency is true
not only of Wisconsin and perhaps northern United
States, but also of other countries. Conceived of on a
socioeconomic left-right continuum, parties to the left
have labor-oriented coalition support and campaign on
a group basis, and parties to the right avoid group appeals and construct a nongroup approach.

On the basis of the data presented in this chapter,
it is possible to speculate that there is an underlying
continuum of races faced by candidates, a continuum
of "security of position." It is already customary in the
literature to think of this continuum in terms of the
party identifications of the voters in a given district. A
Democrat running in a district in which Democrats have
won by an average of 70 percent of the votes in the last
few years is considered a secure or safe candidate. Although party identification is important, it is not all that
contributes to security of position. In addition to (or
perhaps instead of) being the candidate of the majority
party in the district, a candidate may build a coalition
of groups that is powerful enough to keep him in office.
Again, lacking both majority party status or group-
based coalitions, a candidate may still win and maintain
himself in office by establishing a high degree of personal popularity. So there are at least three components
of security of position: the party identifications of the
voters in the district, the candidate's supporting coali-

tion, and the candidate's own personal popularity. Perhaps more could be added.

A candidate at one end of this security of position continuum is quite secure because he has achieved at least one of the following: the party identification of a majority of the voters in the district is identical to his; he has built a coalition of groups in the district sufficient to elect him; he has established a remarkable degree of personal popularity—or any combination of these. A candidate at the other end of the continuum is relatively helpless: he is of the minority party, without significant group support, and unknown.

The data on coalition support presented here suggest that campaign strategies adopted by the candidates vary according to their place on this underlying continuum of security of position. Those candidates relatively near the "secure" end concentrate on bolstering the support they already enjoy: they appeal to the groups in their coalitions, they campaign in their strong areas and neglect their weak areas. Candidates at the other end of the continuum tend to construct an undifferentiated individual appeal rather than an appeal to particular groups within their districts, and also tend to go to their areas of weakness more than secure candidates. At the very ends of the continuum, it may be that candidates adopt plans that are less than efficient for gaining support. The extremely secure candidates, content that they will win in any foreseeable event, do not simply bolster their support but also engage in a campaign to "educate" others. The hopeless candidates, on the other hand, confident that they will lose, decide to "speak their minds" instead of attempting to expand their base of support.

One could also argue that these strategic adaptations to security of position are optimal, that the "rational" candidate (that is, the one who is interested in getting as many votes as he can at as little cost as possible) will calculate in this way. Such an argument would imply that the campaign folklore rules that presumably apply to *all* candidates do not give the candidate enough guidance; he should also assess his place on the security of position continuum and calculate his strategies accordingly.

Thus far, we have drawn conclusions about candidates without regard for the type of office being sought. But type of office has an impact on campaign strategy. In particular, some offices have greater potential for public and mass media attention than others. This appears to be one reason why candidates for the state legislature present issues in a general fashion and consider the characteristics of their audience directly, whereas candidates for higher-level offices adapt their issue presentations to the media. Not only are fewer voters and media people interested in a candidate for the state legislature than in one for the governorship or Congress, but use of the mass media for a state legislative candidacy is also expensive and wasteful in the sense that the medium—television especially—covers a much larger area than the district involved in the election.

Finally, we have observed the impact of the candidate's policy values on his campaign appeals, particularly on his choice of issues. In several ways, however, this impact is greater among Republicans than among Democrats. Although a close race moderates Democratic liberal campaign stands, for instance, it does not have this effect on Republican conservative issue choices. Again, those who emphasize conservative issue positions are more likely to say that they do so for policy reasons than are those who stress liberal ones. All these pieces of information may be considered indications of a greater degree of electoral pragmatism among Democratic candidates.

Some of this effect may be due to the particular

election being studied here: that of 1964. Throughout the campaign, the Presidential candidate of the Republican party, Barry Goldwater, was well known for "standing up for principle regardless of the electoral consequences." The Wisconsin data suggest that some of this frame of mind extended deep into the Republican party, at least to the state legislative level. Whether this phenomenon is transient, occurring only in 1964 and then only because of an unusual Presidential candidate, or a chronic condition of the Republican party is a question that must be settled by future research on other elections and in other contexts.

NOTES

1. One recent book in this category is Stanley Kelley, Jr., *Political Campaigning: Problems in Creating an Informed Electorate* (Washington: The Brookings Institution, 1960).

2. An example is Marshall Loeb and William Safire, *Plunging Into Politics* (New York: McKay, 1964).

3. M. Kent Jennings and L. Harmon Zeigler (eds.), *The Electoral Process* (Englewood Cliffs, N.J.: Prentice-Hall, 1966), has several chapters on campaign strategy: Froman, pp. 1–20, deals with tactics that "all candidates *can* employ," (p. 17, italics mine), for example, and Kessel, pp. 290–304, develops a game strategy for 1960.

4. The argument that campaigns are not normally important has been made by Lewis A. Froman, Jr., *Congressmen and Their Constituencies* (Chicago: Rand McNally, 1963), chap. 4. See also his chapter in M. Kent Jennings and L. Harmon Zeigler, *op. cit.*

5. Leon D. Epstein, *Votes and Taxes* (Madison: Institute of Governmental Affairs, University of Wisconsin Extension Division, 1964).

6. See, for example, William J. Gore and Robert L. Peabody, "The Functions of the Political Campaign: A Case Study," *Western Political Quarterly,* 11 (1958), 55–70.

7. The effect of party on concentration of effort remains when the variable of election chances is controlled, and the effect of election chances also remains when party is controlled.

8. Lewis A. Froman, Jr., *People and Politics* (Englewood Cliffs, N.J.: Prentice-Hall, 1962), p. 96.

9. No differences were found between winners and losers. The differences were between decisive and marginal districts, as indicated in the table.

10. The effect of type of office on issue presentation remains when type of race (decisive or marginal win or loss) is controlled, as does the effect of type of race when office is controlled.

Chapter 6

CONCLUSIONS

★

Throughout this book, references have been made to possible implications that the findings might have for our understanding of the relationships between politicians in democracies and those whom they would represent. This final chapter, while not a summary of the findings of this book, will return in a rather speculative vein to some of the subjects presented at the outset. It is addressed to the question "What do these findings suggest about democratic political systems?"

IMPLICATIONS OF THE FINDINGS

We will begin with some of the implications that this research might have for the conduct of politics in different contexts. Some candidates run for the state legislature, and others run for Congress. Some run in sparsely populated areas, others in more heavily settled areas. Some are Democrats, others Republicans. It has

been shown that politicians' beliefs and strategies do
differ from one context to another. Let us draw together these differences and indicate what consequences
they might have.

Level of Office. The pattern of politics at the state
legislative level is quite different from that in the arena
of statewide offices or Congress. Candidates running for
the state legislature, first, see the office as one of relatively low visibility. They have a lower estimate of voter
interest and information than higher-level candidates
do, a lower estimate of voter issue and candidate awareness, and a greater emphasis on simple party label as
important in accounting for electoral decisions. Also,
the higher-level candidates are believed to get top
billing in the press. Candidates for Congress and statewide offices give a more favorable report of their newspaper support than do those running for the state legislature. This is especially true among Democrats and
among losers, the groups of candidates that would be
most likely to suffer from poor exposure. Politicians at
the state legislative level, furthermore, use more informal means of gathering information about their constituents. Virtually all opinion polling is done at the
higher level, and the higher-level politicians are much
more aware of the possibility that communications
reaching them through their own organization are likely
to be biased. State legislative candidates are relatively
cut off from voter attention, direct information about
voters, and channels of access to rank-and-file citizens.

There is another salient feature of state legislative
districts with important consequences: compared with
congressional or statewide districts, they are much
smaller, geographically and according to population.
Besides being smaller, the state legislative districts are
also likely to be more socially homogeneous, with less
diversity in types of economic or other groupings in

the district at large and in the politician's supporting coalition as well. Once the state legislator gets into office, he is likely to have fewer different groups within his district to whom he must pay attention. This is probably why, among winners only, state legislators are more likely than higher-level officeholders to state that one group within their supporting coalition is most important to their election chances, that an interest group is most important to them, and that they feel they must keep someone in their district satisfied in order to win. One reasonable inference one may draw from these findings is that a state legislator, more than a congressman or a holder of a statewide office, takes account of the crucial members of his supporting coalition in the making of public policy. Because he believes that they are so important to him in terms of his reelection chances, he cannot afford to slight them as much as could a representative who does not place as great an importance upon them.

This line of reasoning is consistent with the greater isolation of state legislators from voters and the media. State legislators feel their office is one of low visibility for the public at large. This feeling leaves them free to deal with interest groups and others in the state capitol with less regard for their rank-and-file constituents than a congressman might feel, and it makes resistance to demands from interest groups and others on the grounds that voters will punish them more difficult. This combination of beliefs about the environment may have something to do with the tendency that other writers have postulated for interest groups to be stronger and more active in state legislatures than in Congress.[1] At least in their dealings with organized labor and the groups like lodges and educators that are classified as non-economic, state legislators are more prone than higher-level officials to say that the group expects something of them in return for their support. This piece of evidence would again fit with the notion that interest groups bulk somewhat larger in the thinking of state legislators and in their decision-making than they do for congressmen.

In addition to these postulated differences in the behavior of representatives once in office, there are demonstrable differences between office levels in campaign strategy. In general, the campaigns of state legislative candidates are much less based on the mass media than those for higher-level office. Even if a legislative candidate could afford a good deal of media coverage (most cannot) it might still be wasteful since it would be likely to reach constituents other than his own, and even his own constituents might take no notice of this kind of publicity. Any talk of public policy issues in their campaigns, furthermore, tends to be more general and vague than in a campaign for higher-level office, partly because they see their constituents as less interested in policy than a congressman does and partly because they are not obliged to vary their appeal day by day in order to place stories in the newspapers.

In sum, we may postulate that the differences between congressmen's and state legislators' views of their political worlds result in differences between them in their relationships with their constituencies. At the state legislative level, a politician is probably more inexperienced and hence more at sea than the average congressional candidate or incumbent. He casts about for sources of guidance for his decisions on campaigning and on weighty matters of governmental policy should he be elected. Unlike the congressman, he feels that voters are not involved in politics at his governmental level and that the media do not cover his activities as fully. He feels much less visible than his colleagues in higher-level office, and he has less direct, personal strength with voters. Because of this situation, he feels he must place more reliance on interest groups than a congressman is likely to do.

In contrast, the candidate for Congress or a state-wide office is more likely to feel that voters are paying attention to what he does, that the mass media will cover his actions, and that his constituents are looking at his policy-making record. To the extent that a representative behaves toward his constituents through his anticipation of their reactions to the various alternatives from which he might choose, therefore, the congressional politician is more likely to take account of media and voter reaction in the construction of his campaign strategies and in the making of his public policy stands. His tendency in this direction, we might further hypothesize, is reinforced by the congressman's feeling that his own policy-making behavior will make a difference at the polls, in contrast to the state legislator's inclination to believe that his elections are decided less according to his personal actions in office. With more personal strength with the voters, a congressman feels he has less need for interest-group leaders and is more on his own. Because he believes that voters and media are paying greater attention to his pronouncements, furthermore, the candidate for Congress is more likely than the state legislative candidate to campaign on relatively specific issues of governmental policy and even to give a more ideological cast to his comments about politics.

Area of State.   The two areas of Wisconsin cited in this book—the relatively urban southeast and the more sparsely populated northwest—have been used to indicate differing types of districts. We have discovered some interesting differences between the two areas of the state that hint at some salient features of their politics.

It appears that in several senses, the relatively small-town and rural area of the state is less highly politicized than the more densely populated portion. When assessing the reasons for their coalition members' support, for example, politicians in the more sparsely populated northwest section are much more likely to cite personal reasons like long-standing friendship or approval of their integrity. Politicians in the relatively urban southeast section, however, tend more to cite matters of public policy such as the agreement between candidate and supporter on some type of legislation. Not only are relatively urban politicians more policy-oriented, but they also believe more than candidates in small towns and rural areas that their supporters expect something of them in return for support. An exception in the rural northwest section are the farmers, from whom the politicians quite naturally feel demands. Candidates in the southeast section, however, are more likely in general to say that coalition building is a "support in return for favors" arrangement.

In addition to being more politicized in these senses, the more densely populated area of the state is more polarized according to the business-labor distinction than the small-town and rural areas. Republicans in the southeast section are prone to list a business-oriented coalition of supporters, and Democrats there are prone to cite organized labor as important in their coalitions. Among politicians in the more small-town and rural northwest section, however, it is much more common to find a coalition that includes both business and labor or neither of these two groups. The labor-business dichotomy, in short, is much more in evidence in the more densely populated area of the state.

Experts who make demographic predictions tell us that over the next few years the population of the United States will become increasingly concentrated in metropolitan areas and their immediate environs. If this is true, and if these areas are more like the southeast section of Wisconsin than like the northwest section, we might speculate that the character of politics will also change. For good or ill, politics is likely to become increasingly policy-oriented. Electoral coalitions are more likely to be built on at least a tacit understanding of support in return for legislative decisions or other official favors, rather than on a "friends and neighbors" personal approach. And perhaps most significant, the politics of the nation are likely to become more polarized between business and labor, and more broadly, between those of higher and lower social status. As people live closer to one another and become more interdependent, the result is not always closer cooperation. In fact, increased interaction may accentuate fundamental differences. For instance, suburbs and inner cities are forced to interact in some fashion, and the result is not always accord.

At any rate, we have seen that a policy-charged, *quid pro quo,* polarized kind of politics is characteristic of the more densely populated area of Wisconsin. It would seem a reasonable conjecture that as the United States becomes more urbanized, its politics will increasingly take on this character.

Political Parties. Although party voting in American legislatures is not as impressively regular as it is in the British House of Commons, studies of roll calls have discovered a good deal of party influence on voting. Whatever party regularity one does discover is clearly not enforced by any belief on the part of the legislators that the party organization is indispensable in their fight for reelection. Only one winning candidate in this study stated that the party was the most important member of his coalition.

This book has set forth a relatively simple explanation for party differences in the United States: that they are rooted in differences of coalition support. The evidence for this proposition is striking. Not a single Democrat in this study perceived his supporting coalition as including business and professional groups but not labor, and not a single Republican listed a coalition which included organized labor but not business and professional people. There is a constituency factor imbedded in the social structure, then, that helps to explain party differences.

This relationship between interest groups and political parties corresponds at least roughly to the alignments one finds in the electorate. From the earliest voting studies on, it has been commonly discovered that higher-status groups have tended to identify with and vote for Republicans and that lower-status groups have tended to identify with and vote for Democrats. Not only do members of these electoral groupings behave in this way, but they also tend to perceive the parties as representing different elements of society. A majority of the voters at least view some sort of group benefits as following from the election of one party rather than another. The Democratic party is seen as the party of lower-status groups, whereas the Republican party is seen as the opposite.[2] This book adds evidence that these voter perceptions reflect the actual state of affairs at the elite level.

We have noted in several contexts the special place of organized labor in the Democratic party. Although there is of course no formal connection between the two such as there is in the case of the Labour party in Britain, there is still a heavy informal involvement. Organized labor, first of all, is believed to be more interested in questions of public policy than are other types of supporters, perhaps because labor makes its positions so abundantly clear. Governmental policy-makers, then, may take labor's views into account more than they do the assumed views of a group that is perceived to be less interested in policy. Also, Democratic candidates tend more than Republicans to obtain campaign finances directly from an interest group (organized labor), whereas Republican contributors are more likely to channel their funds through the party organization. When asked which of their supporters is most important to them in terms of election chances, furthermore, Democrats are more likely to opt for organized labor than Republicans are to choose business or professional people. This importance of labor to Democrats is especially true of politicians at the state legislative level. Many Republicans at this level, especially unsuccessful candidates, feel that their party organization is virtually their only friend: some Democrats feel this way about labor.

The majority of Democratic candidates, however, are not so directly tied to organized labor. Only a minority, in other words, maintain intimate connections with labor and come to rely on them for finances, campaign workers, and eventually votes. In another sense as well, labor cannot be said to "control" the Democratic party. "Control" implies that the group would somehow get the politician to make a decision other than one which he would have made had the group not influenced him. But it could very well be, as several respondents indicated, that Democrats would choose the same policy direction, organized labor or no. Indeed, labor was not seen by candidates to "expect" anything in return for support any more than any other group, perhaps because, as one politician put it, "They never had to ask." And no party differences emerged when the candidates were asked if there was someone in their districts they felt they had to keep satisfied in order to win.

On the basis of these data, organized labor cannot fairly be said to "control" Democratic candidates. It does, however, occupy a more central place in Democratic politics than similar interest groups do for the other party. Republican candidates do, of course, readily acknowledge the support of business and professional groups, but they do not seem to be so explicitly tied to these groups as the Democrats are apparently tied to organized labor.

Party differences in coalition support have their impact on campaign decisions. Democrats are at something of an advantage in that they have the potential support of labor groups and of the identifiable ethnic, religious, and racial minority groups. They make group appeals when they campaign, whereas Republicans—at a disadvantage with the more numerous subgroups in the population—tend to gloss over group differences, avoid appealing to distinct groups within the electorate, and attempt simply to reach voters as individuals without regard for their group affiliations. Group appeals, then, are far from being a universal stock in trade among politicians; in fact, Republicans avoid them.

The parties are also noticeably different in the issue appeals that they direct at the electorate. Democrats tend to discuss "liberal" issues like welfare, civil rights, and education, whereas Republicans tend to discuss "conservative" issues like the size of government budgets, the need for efficiency in government, and taxation incentives for business activity. The three variables of party, coalition support, and campaign strategy are closely associated.

In addition to their impact on campaign strategy, it would be reasonable to assume that these party differences in coalitions affect the decisions politicians make on public policy questions once they get into office. An elected official's sympathetic understanding is probably sooner given for the problems of his active supporters than for those of his active opponents. Given the party differences in supporting coalitions, then, which party gains office is important since it probably determines which groups will have the easier access to governmental decision-makers. If a Democrat wins, labor will have an easier time of it; if a Republican wins, business and professional groups will normally have the advantage. In terms of democratic theory, different constituencies are being represented depending upon which party wins.

Election Outcome.   A major hypothesis with which this study began was that candidates' beliefs and strategies might help to account for success or failure at the polls. Perhaps those candidates who win have a more sophisticated notion of electoral forces than those who lose. Perhaps they adopt a particularly clever kind of campaign strategy. In short, there might be something about the way in which they calculate that would contribute to the outcome.

Far from discovering such a difference, we have found that the election outcome has a profound *effect* upon politicians' beliefs. Winners tend to congratulate both themselves (on a well-run campaign) and the voters (on their perceptive, intelligent judgments). Losers tend to rationalize their defeat by attributing it to factors beyond their control and by deprecating the voters' interest in politics, their level of information, and their ability to judge election issues. This congratulation-rationalization effect occurs not only after the election, but also to an extent before the voters go to the polls, since many candidates anticipate what the eventual outcome will be. In any event, after examining the data presented in this book, it would be difficult to maintain that politicians normally win because of some more clever or sophisticated calculation about the electorate.

It is not, of course, true that campaign strategy never makes a difference. A highly successful campaign, one effective in winning votes, may be planned and executed without a great deal of knowledge about how voters make up their minds. Indeed, most campaigns may be aimed at such elites as interest-group leaders and newspaper writers and at the attentive public, on the assumption that the thrust of the campaign will seep down to rank-and-file voters. And perhaps because the office is visible or because the attentive public passes cues down, the campaign may indeed get through.

The congratulation-rationalization effect may have important implications for the behavior of politicians once they attain public office. It appears that because of their electoral victory incumbent officeholders overestimate the degree to which people in their districts pay attention to them. If an elected politician feels that the public is watching him (the public upon which he depends for his job and his political life), we might hypothesize that he will take his constituents' likely views into account in making his policy decisions more than if he did not believe they were attentive. In fact, I have presented elsewhere evidence which suggests that this is indeed so.[3] If there were no congratulation-rationalization effect, incumbent officeholders would have a lower estimate of voter involvement in politics than they do. It is likely, therefore, that this effect increases the influence constituencies have on representatives.

Incumbent officeholders exhibit another tendency not shared by their less successful opponents. Perhaps because they have had recent experience with occupying a governmental position, they tend to be more cognizant of interest-group demands and are more likely to believe that these groups are important in electoral politics. Again, this occurs especially at the state legislative level. Elected state legislators are more likely than are their opponents (or candidates at the higher level) to believe that an interest group is most important to them in terms of their election chances. This belief is in contrast to their attitude toward the political party organization: they are much less likely than their opponents to feel that the party is their most important coalition member. State legislative winners are also more likely to feel that they must keep someone satisfied in order to win. Thus, any tendency to believe that interest groups are important is concentrated where it counts, in a policy sense: among incumbent officeholders.

We have also noted in several contexts that the closeness of the race has an impact on beliefs and strategies. For certain campaign decisions, there appears to be some adaptation of strategy to the likely voting behavior of the district in which the candidate seeks office. Decisive losers—those who got less than 45 percent of the two-party vote—concentrate on the areas in their districts in which they feel that they would otherwise run poorly, perhaps because they have few areas in their districts in which they would run well. Among decisive winners, those who feel uncertain about the election outcome despite their secure position concentrate on their strong areas, as a kind of bolstering strategy, whereas those who feel sure of the outcome experiment a bit, concentrating more on their weak areas. Candidates running in decisive districts, furthermore, tend to keep their issue presentation general, perhaps because they feel that neither the mass media nor voters are paying much attention to their race anyway and that detailed policy discussion would only bore them.

Once they get into office, decisive winners are more likely than marginal winners to say that they must keep someone in their districts satisfied in order to win. Their unsuccessful opponents say the same. Probably because they are faced with rather one-sided, relatively homogeneous districts, there is in fact one electoral grouping that dominates the district's politics, and the candidates recognize this. Once they have satisfied this group, they also tend to feel more than politicians in marginal districts that they can afford to ignore the demands of other groups.

One might expect, finally, that the actual outcome of the race would be related to the subjective uncertainty of the politician. That is to say, the candidates running in races that are won by lopsided margins would feel more sure of the eventual election outcome than those in close districts. Although there is a relationship between uncertainty and actual election outcome, it is not very strong. Considerable numbers of decisive winners and losers still feel uncertain about the outcome of the election. The candidates who feel most uncertain are the marginal winners, those who won by a close vote and face another campaign for reelection. Some degree of uncertainty is probably functional for a politician; it keeps him and his staff on their toes and working hard at the business of staying in office.

REPRESENTATION IN DEMOCRACIES

To reiterate a fundamental point made in the first chapter, it is vitally important to distinguish between average voters within a politician's district and the political elites. The bulk of rank-and-file voters are characterized by a minimal involvement in politics and by few explicit demands upon officeholders in government. Political elites, however, such as interest-group leaders, party activists, newspaper editors, and those concerned enough to write the politician a letter, are more heavily involved in politics, and do make explicit demands. Indeed, an "elite" may be defined in terms of high political involvement. Even though politicians often mix the two, it is important to make a conceptual distinction.

It is possible for representation in democracies to take place by a process of explicit communications between the politicians and the people. A concerned citizen, for example, may write his congressman, who may take account of his and others' letters in his deliberations on weighty matters of public policy. Or the public, at least the attentive public, may decide on the basis of the information at their disposal that the congressman is not representing them and throw the rascal out.

From studies of voting behavior, we know that in the communications which flow from politicians to rank-and-file citizens, information is transmitted through a variety of channels. The mass media, for instance, cover political events, thereby transmitting political information to any citizens who might be paying attention. Political cues are also passed on by more attentive members of the public to the less attentive.[4] Average citizens have no direct contact with politicians and depend instead upon these channels for their information about politicians.

The same might be said of the politicians. They have very little direct contact with rank-and-file voters. Whatever interaction they have with people from their districts takes place with members of political elites. A local labor union official comes to call. A party precinct captain sets up a coffee hour primarily attended by activists. A newspaper editor writes an editorial. On the rare occasions that he does get out to rub elbows with "the people," the contacts are fleeting and largely devoid of policy content. Average citizens, in sum, are distant from the politician.

This distance from rank-and-file voters creates something of a dilemma for politicians, for their political life depends on the approval of a majority of such voters at the polls. How do they resolve this dilemma?

Some politicians develop fairly direct sources of information about voters. Most candidates at least do some analysis of past election statistics in their districts to see in a rough way what the election behavior of voters is and what areas within the district are strong or weak. Those politicians who can afford it and who have the inclination take polls of various kinds. The polls may range from extremely unreliable mail questionnaires or supermarket polls to commercial surveys of varying quality. But polls worth the expense in time and money are beyond the financial reach of most candidates for the state legislature and even of many candidates for Congress. Other politicians try to get a feel for their constituents' thinking by judging the warmth or coolness of the reception they get as they move among the people in campaign periods or at other times.

The candidate does not usually deem his own party organization a reliable source of information about the electorate. The problem here is that although the candidate does hear a good deal about how an election is going from party activists, he feels that due in part to the activists' desire to encourage him, the information they transmit will be biased. Politicians interpret cues coming to them in terms of the source, then, and apply a discount factor to information coming from sources thought to be unreliable. Communication bias is recognized and corrected.

Aside from using elites as transmitters of information from average citizens, politicians pay direct attention to the elites' expression of their own policy views. Many politicians may do this more or less because there simply are no other sources of information and demands from the district. Unable either to get through to the bulk of voters or to receive any meaningful information about their wishes, politicians turn to those in their districts who *are* making their demands known and who will be watching their policy-making behavior. They listen and respond to interest-group leaders, party leaders, media people, and those who take the trouble to write letters. These are the constituents whom representatives and candidates for office are able to learn something about and can hope to influence.

Some politicians may deal with these elites in the hope that the elites are representative of the electorate at large. If this assumption is correct, then actions in response to elite demands should have the same effect as do actions based upon more specific knowledge of rank-and-file wishes ascertainable only by more strenuous and costly effort. Other politicians may believe that by satisfying the elites, not only will approval be forthcoming from them, but this approval will also seep down through the electorate by means of opinion leadership. If nobody among the important leaders is dissatisfied, these politicians reason, then displeasure will hardly be widespread among average citizens. Other politicians, perhaps most of them, pay close attention to the elites simply because these groups are important in their own right. After all, they furnish finances, campaign workers, and perhaps their influence with certain blocs of voters, all important political commodities. Aside from the possible value of the political elite as a kind of surrogate for voters, then, its members are crucial to the politician for their own sake.

Up to this point, discussion has centered on the influence of a constituency upon the politician through direct communication: letters, visits, lobbying, and so forth. But another, much more subtle, way in which constituents influence representatives is through the rule of anticipated reactions.[5] A politician not only responds to the direct communications from those who are important to him, but he also tries to anticipate the reactions of these people to each of the several courses of action open to him. When he does this, it can be said that the constituency has exerted an influence on the politician because his anticipation of their response to his actions has altered his likely course.

The findings discussed in this book bear on the ways in which a representative might anticipate the reactions of his constituents, both average citizens and political elites. First, the politician (and especially the politician who is finally elected to public office) believes that voters are aware of his actions. Incumbent officeholders, we have discovered, tend to congratulate the electorate and thus to overestimate the degree of voter involvement and issue consciousness. This tendency, I would suggest, makes it more likely that the politician will attempt to anticipate voters' reactions to his policy decisions than if he did not believe they were paying attention to him.

Uncertainty about the effects of his actions adds to this tendency to take account of his constituents' likely reactions. If a politician had complete knowledge of the electoral consequences of his actions, he would know that many types of behavior would not affect his stock with voters appreciably, would recognize that a few would, and would also know which actions would hurt him and which would not. As it is, however, politicians cannot be that certain. Even if they run for "safe" seats, they still may face potentially ruinous primary opposition. The politician, therefore, is obliged to behave *as if* his actions had electoral consequences—whether they do or not in fact—in order to provide the little extra margin that could be crucial. Uncertainty about the reactions of the electorate, then, may serve the function of making representatives more sensitive to the probable wishes of their constituents.

As noted above, however, most politicians have few direct lines of communication with rank-and-file citizens. Much of the anticipation of constituents' responses, then, takes place at the elite level. Political elites are constituents with whom politicians have some contact and about whom they have some knowledge. It is much simpler to take their probable reactions into account than to attempt direct contact with average voters. The same reasons for politicians' reactions to explicit elite demands stated above also apply to anticipated reactions.

Because acting in anticipation of constituents' reactions is one kind of representation in democracies, it appears that different segments of society are represented in government depending upon which party is successful in its quest for office. The dramatic differences between the parties in coalition support discussed in this study go a long way toward explaining party differences observed in legislative voting, and these differences in coalition support also have implications for representation. If a Democrat wins the election, the chances are that organized labor and racial and ethnic minority groups will have greater representation in the councils of government than will business or professional groups. The obverse applies for the Republican: if he wins, the odds are that business and professional groups will be able to bend his ear more than will organized labor. There are at least two constituencies, then, divided roughly along social status lines within most electoral districts, and these constituencies are represented differently depending on which candidate wins.

All this discussion, of course, does not imply that a politician is strictly bound in by his constituency or even by his supporting coalition in his choice of campaign strategies and governmental policy alternatives. Even in their relationships with elites, most politicians do not see coalition building as a *quid pro quo* arrangement of support in return for favors, and most politicians do not believe that any one group within their district aside from their campaign workers is absolutely indispensable to their election victory. About half the candidates also believe that groups support them for reasons of public policy, so only this half would have reason to take into account the likely policy views of these groups. The proportion of politicians who believe that groups support them for policy reasons is greater among Democrats and politicians above the state legislative level.

There is a limit, then, to the extent to which constituencies are likely to influence politicians—some room for other factors beside constituency opinion to contribute to the politicians' decisions. His own policy values, for instance, are important determinants of his decisions. Most candidates run for office with some views on government policy that naturally play a part in their decisions once in office and also influence their choice of issues to discuss in the campaign. Communications from such other actors in the system as party leaders, heads of state, and the executive branch of government, also can affect the legislator. The demands and probable policy views of constituents, therefore, although surely important to the politician, should not be taken as the sole determinants of his behavior.

NOTES

1. See Lester W. Milbrath, *The Washington Lobbyists* (Chicago: Rand McNally, 1963), pp. 301–04.

2. For evidence on these points, see Bernard Berelson *et al., Voting* (Chicago: University of Chicago Press, 1954), chaps. 4 and 5; and Angus Campbell, Philip E. Converse, Warren E. Miller, and Donald E. Stokes, *The American Voter* (New York: Wiley, 1960), chaps. 10, 12, and 13.

3. John W. Kingdon, "Politicians' Beliefs about Voters," *American Political Science Review*, 61 (1967), 137, note 3.

4. Berelson, *et al., op. cit.*, pp. 109 ff.

5. Carl J. Friedrich, *Constitutional Government and Democracy* (Boston: Ginn, 1950), p. 49.

APPENDIX A

Some Methodological Considerations

This study was run generally as a standard interviewing project, using most of the rules and procedures that by now have become familiar to students of the social sciences. As such, the research fell into the following stages: sample selection, construction and pretesting of the interview schedule, production or field interviewing, coding, data processing, and analysis. All these steps were executed by the author.

SELECTION OF THE SAMPLE

The sample of respondents interviewed in this study was chosen in two ways. First, half of the sample is composed of a census of the 1964 Wisconsin candidates[1] for the following offices: United States senator, United States representative, governor, lieutenant governor, secretary of state, state treasurer, and state attorney general. All the candidates for Congress and the statewide elective offices in 1964, then, were in the sample.

The other half of the sample was composed of candidates for the state senate and assembly. All these candi-

[1] In two districts that had terms longer than two years (one for United States senator and one for state senator), the 1962 candidates were chosen.

dates could not be interviewed for lack of time, so a sample of legislative districts was drawn at the ratio of 1 in 8 in order to equal the number of candidates for the higher-level offices mentioned above, and both the winning and losing candidate in each of the chosen districts were interviewed.

To be certain that the districts chosen were not concentrated disproportionately in one or two areas of the state, the sample of legislators was stratified by geographical area, which approximates a stratification by population density because the southeastern portion of the state is more densely populated than the northwestern area. The four strata, with equal numbers of senate and assembly districts in each, were (1) Milwaukee County; (2) the southeast part of the state, which includes Madison, Racine, Kenosha, and Sheboygan; (3) the Fox River valley and central Wisconsin, which includes Green Bay, Fond du Lac, Wausau, and Baraboo; and (4) the north and west. Legislative districts within each of these strata were chosen with a table of random numbers.

This sample selection has the virtue of obtaining an even spread on all four of the basic independent variables described in Chapter 1. Choosing the winner and loser in each district, first of all, not only guarantees that winner-loser comparisons may be made without fear of possible spurious relationships showing up due to candidates' coming from different districts, but also provides equal numbers of winners and losers, Republicans and Democrats. The sample of legislative candidates was chosen deliberately to equal the number of higher-level candidates, and the stratification procedure ensures an equal distribution by area of the state. Especially because the sample is so small, even distributions on these variables is a decided advantage: it enables the researcher to make cross-tabulations that are percentaged on as high a number of cases as possible, so that the likelihood of prohibitively small cell frequencies is minimized.

A summary statement of the sample appears in Table A-1. The total of 66 was eventually reduced by 4. Of the Assembly candidates, 2 had no general election opponents,

TABLE A-1

Composition of the Sample

OFFICE	DISTRICTS	INDIVIDUALS
U.S. senator	2	4
U.S. congressman	10	20
Statewide offices	5	10
State senator	4	8
State assemblyman	12	24
Total	33	66

and of the statewide candidates, 2 refused to grant an interview. A total of 62 individuals, then, were actually interviewed, plus 8 pretest respondents.

Rate of Return. The fact that 62 out of 64 individuals on the list were interviewed means that a 97 percent rate of return was achieved. One reason for this excellent rate of return was that I simply did not write off a respondent unless he told me flatly that he would never grant an interview. Most respondents consented readily to making an appointment and kept it. There were a few broken appointments and a few individuals would not set a time and place. Most respondents, however, were extremely cooperative and punctual.

Statistical Tests. No use was made of statistical tests of significance or estimation procedures in this study. An excellent summary of the reasons for this decision, most of them having to do with sampling, can be found in an appendix to Lipset, Trow, and Coleman's *Union Democracy.*[2] I apply their argument to the present case as follows:

For reasons of manageability, my sample size is rela-

[2] Seymour Martin Lipset, Martin Trow, and James Coleman, *Union Democracy* (New York: Free Press, 1956), appendix 1, part B.

tively small by statistical standards. It is conceivable that large percentage differences could appear in the tables which, solely because of the small sample size, would not be statistically significant. By the rules involved in such procedures, these findings would be discarded. This might result in the dismissal of some propositions that would be of interest and use to students of this and related subjects. It is therefore probably more useful simply to state the results in percentage tables, generalize on the basis of them concerning other candidates for office, and invite replication of the study under different conditions. Especially since the study is exploratory, and I believe that casting the net wide is in this case more important than statistical significance.

Furthermore, the data analysis began by simply running the four independent variables against everything else to see what results would obtain. Hypotheses were thus developed from the data themselves, and it would have been tautological to test these hypotheses on the same data. Hypothesis-testing is, however, what tests of significance are designed to accomplish; for this reason, they are inappropriate in this study.

I am aware that there is considerable disagreement among social scientists over significance testing. This was the research decision made for this study, however, and it is important to state the reasons for it. I should add that most of the differences in the major tables presented in this book would be statistically significant anyway, but the fact that it happened to turn out this way should not affect the decision to use the tests or not.

THE INTERVIEW

A structured interview was used in this research, with the same questions asked of each respondent in the same order. Standard ways of rephrasing questions when necessary were also developed, and standard nonleading probes were used. The most significant advantage of this technique is that it enables the researcher to compare one respondent with another with some degree of assurance that their responses were elicited by the same stimulus. This comparability is crucial to any attempt at determining the frequency with which a given response is made, as well as identifying relationships among variables. A simple cross-tabulation, for instance, is a comparison of two or more groups along a given variable, and its validity depends on the ability to compare cases.

One of course pays some cost for opting for any particular technique. One drawback of a structured interview is that some interesting tangents may not be fully explored because of the desire to complete the questionnaire and to treat respondents alike. This cost was recognized and deliberately paid because of the judgment that comparable and complete answers to all the questions of interest were more important. Another penalty of a structured interview is that the schedule is not adapted to the individual capabilities and knowledge of the respondents. I felt that this consideration was not so crucial here, since all were candidates and thus had enough in common for the same interview schedule to be used universally. Here as in all research, the technique to be used should be adapted to the particular research problem.

Within the constraint of a structured interview, various kinds of questions were used. Some were open-ended and invited the individual to speak as he wished; others were of the fixed-alternative type. In each case, however, the questions were worded in and delivered from memory in an informal conversational manner in order to make the interview as comfortable as possible for the candidate—and at the same time preserve the feature of comparability.

Recording Responses. Once the decision on degree of structure is made, the method by which the interviewee's responses will be recorded remains to be decided. Recording methods in social science research have ranged all the way from taking no notes and taping memories of the interview immediately afterward to taping the interviews themselves. I rejected both these alternatives. I felt that taking no notes and trusting to memory would not yield the detailed information desired and would probably result in incomplete records of the interviews which would not be capable of comparison. The gain in terms of rapport, I decided, would not be worth the cost for my research purposes. Taping the actual interview, on the other hand, might reduce the frankness with which some respondents would speak. So I opted for writing in the interview. I recorded the responses as nearly verbatim as possible without making the respondents wait for uncomfortably long periods, and wrote up the interview in the respondents' own words from these notes immediately afterward. The goal was to obtain the required information in a complete and accurate form, and yet to make the respondent feel as relaxed as possible.

Interviewing Conditions.   Interviews were held throughout the state of Wisconsin and in Washington. The typical interview, uninterrupted except for an occasional telephone call, was held in the respondent's office. Two-thirds of the interviews were in offices, and another one-sixth were in the respondents' homes. The remaining interviews were held under widely varying conditions—in bars, across counters in business places, over dinner, in automobiles, and walking down halls. The conduct of these interviews under less than desirable conditions was due either to my desire to be accommodating and to adapt to an interview situation in which the respondent would be most comfortable or to my judgment that the interview had to be taken under these conditions or not at all. Most interviews, however, were held under nearly ideal circumstances: in an office or home, with few interruptions, and with no one else present.

Regardless of the circumstances, respondents almost without exception were friendly and cooperative, seemed pleased to discuss the questions openly and completely, and were very generous with their time. The shortest interview, with a respondent who gave unusually clipped answers and

volunteered no incidental information, lasted twenty minutes. The longest was two hours and fifteen minutes. The mean amount of time spent in the interview was approximately one hour.

Pretest. I pretested my interview schedule on eight candidates for the state legislature who resided in or near Madison and who were not in the sample. This pretest was an opportunity for free experimentation with the interview, and I therefore explored various orders and wordings of questions, ways of approaching respondents, and methods of recording their answers. I would take two interviews, revise the schedule, take two more, revise, and so forth, until a satisfactory questionnaire was assembled. The result of the entire process of interview schedule construction and pretesting was the production schedule—the questionnaire actually used—which appears as Appendix B to this book.

Timing. The interviewing was done during the months of March and April, 1965, about five months after the election. The postelection timing allowed the candidates to reflect a bit on the election, but was not so distant from the event that recall would be drastically impaired. Respondents were also more at their leisure than they would have been during the campaign. One largely unanticipated penalty for this choice of timing was that some of the politicians' beliefs evidently change between the preelection and postelection periods, as we have noted throughout this book. In a few instances, therefore, these data may not be strictly applicable to the campaign period itself, though we can use them to make some reasonable inferences about preelection cognitions.

APPENDIX B

Interview Schedule

.. First, let me ask a few background questions. How did you get interested in politics?

!. Have you held any party offices? Which one(s)?

. What was the first elective office you ran for? Why did you decide to run?

If R has run for office before this last time, ask the following questions:

   a. Will you give me a history of the offices you have run for and the outcomes of these campaigns?

   b. **If R was an incumbent before the last election:** How worried were you about being re-elected this time? How vigorously did you campaign?

   c. **If R was not an incumbent before the last election:** Why did you decide to run in this last election?

4. Now let's consider your last campaign for a minute. In this last election, which issues did you emphasize?

   a. Why did you choose these? Did these reasons for choosing issues differ from other elections? [**If yes:** What are other reasons?]

   b. How did you present your chosen issues—did you deal generally with them, or did you treat them in a more detailed fashion? Why did you do it this way?

5. In your campaigning, is there any group or groups of voters that you especially make an appeal to?

   If yes: Which ones are these? Why do you consider them important?

   If no: What *is* your over-all campaign plan, then?

6. Do you concentrate on voters in areas where you think you will do well, or where you think you'll run poorly, or what?

7. **[Show card]*** Consider the three factors at the top of this card. Would you tell me how important each of these is in determining the choice of the voters? You can use the categories at the bottom of the card.

   a. If you were to rank the three factors, which would you say is most important in determining the choice voters will make? Which is second?

   b. Some candidates are considered to be attractive candidates, and others are not. What personal characteristics do you think a strong candidate should have?

8. Generally speaking, would you say that voters in your district are interested in your campaign, or not?

   If interested: Would you say they're *very* interested?

9. Do you think that voters in your district are informed about the way the candidates stand on the issues of the election, or not?

   If informed: Are they *very* well informed?

10. Would you say that voters who consider themselves

* The card shown respondents was as follows:

---

1. Party label
2. Issues of the election
3. Personal characteristics of the candidates

ALL IMPORTANT
VERY IMPORTANT
OF SOME IMPORTANCE
OF LITTLE IMPORTANCE
NOT IMPORTANT

independents are generally *more* or *less* interested and informed about politics than party voters?

11. Now, are you fairly sure you know how well you'll do when the votes are in, or are you more uncertain on that score?

   If sure: Go to question 12.

   If not sure:

   a. What are some reasons for your uncertainty about how you'll do? Anything else?

   b. Do you tend to get a picture of your chances that overestimates your final vote total or underestimates it? Why is that?

12. Can you tell me your sources of information about how you will do when the votes are in?

   Probe ("Anything else?") **to get as complete a list as possible.**

   a. How much do you rely on each of these sources?

13. **For each item on the following list which has not yet been discussed, ask: (1) Does he use it, and (2) how much does he rely on it?**

   1. Analysis of past election statistics in your district
   2. Polls [ask what type of poll, how conducted]
   3. Party organization people
   4. Your own campaign workers and personal staff
   5. Crowds, warmth of reception
   a. Are there any other indicators of how you're doing that we haven't mentioned?

14. Let's turn from rank-and-file voters now, and concentrate on other sorts of groups in your district. Would you tell me first what groups of people supported your candidacy in the last election?

   For each item on the following list which has not yet been mentioned, ask about it:

   1. Interest groups
   2. Party organization activists
   3. Campaign workers and personal staff
   4. Newspapers
   5. Financial contributors

15. 1. Interest groups mentioned
     2. Campaign workers and personal staff
     3. Newspapers mentioned

Ask about each item on the above list <u>individually</u>:

   a. Can you tell me why they support you?
   b. Do you feel that they expect something of you in return for their support? [**If yes:** What do they expect?]

16. Taking this list of supporting groups again, who would you say is most important in terms of your election chances?

   Could you give me 2nd, 3rd, and 4th most important?
   Why do you consider these especially important?

17. I imagine there are some people you must keep satisfied in order to win. Can you tell me who these people are in your case?

Probe for mention of <u>groups</u>.

   a. How do you satisfy them?
   b. Whose demands can you afford to pay less attention to?

18. Finally, let me ask you a couple of very general questions about this whole subject. First, could you summarize the major factors that have contributed to your wins and defeats over the years?

19. Another question—how important is it to you that you be elected, or are there other considerations that enter into your choices?

If there are others:

   a. Are your interest in winning elections and these other considerations normally in conflict?
   b. When you are faced with a conflict between the two alternatives, which comes first?

20. I've asked you many questions during this interview. Is there anything else either relating to the questions we've covered or on another subject that you would like to discuss?

21. Let me just get a little routine information down here.

   a. First, what is your occupation? [**If R is an in-**

cumbent in a full-time position, ask his occupation before entering politics.] What was your father's occupation?

b. What's the last grade of school or year of college you completed? [**Name of college, if applicable.**]
c. What is your church preference?
d. What is your nationality background?
e. May I ask your age? How old were you when you first ran for office?

INDEX